I0007660

Build Your WordPress Website from Scratch

Complete & Detailed Practical Guide
for Non-Techies

About this series
The series "Build And Monetize Your Own WordPress* Website"
includes books and planners written and designed by André Zon.

Books

1. WordPress Website Building 101.
Everything You Need to Know to Get Started.

2. **Build Your WordPress Website from Scratch.**
Complete & Detailed Practical Guide For Non-Techies.

3. Create Content and Do SEO on Your WordPress Website.
Complete & Detailed Practical Guide For Non-Techies.

4. Promote Your WordPress Website Perfectly.
Complete & Detailed Practical Guide For Website Owners.

5. Maintain Your WordPress Website Perfectly.
Complete & Detailed Practical Guide For Website Owners.

6. Monetize Your WordPress Website Perfectly.
Complete & Detailed Practical Guide For Website Owners.

Planners

1. Website Concept Planner.

2. **Website Development Planner** is the companion planner for this book.

3. Website Content Creation Planner.

4. Website Promotion Planner.

5. Website Maintenance Planner.

6. Website Monetization Planner.

Information and news
Actual information about these books and planners
is published and updated on the websites:

https://andrezon.com - author's site.
Please scan this QR code to open it.

https://buildownsite.com - site of the project.
Please scan this QR code to open it.

* The trademark WORDPRESS is used under license from the WordPress Foundation.

Build and Monetize
Your Own WordPress Website

Build Your WordPress Website from Scratch

Complete & Detailed Practical Guide
for Non-Techies

André Zon

André Zon

Build And Monetize Your Own WordPress Website (Series).
Book #2.   Build Your WordPress Website from Scratch.
              Complete & Detailed Practical Guide For Non-Techies.
Edition 2024.

The trademark WORDPRESS is used under license from the WordPress Foundation.

This book is a practical guide to creating a WordPress-based website from scratch.

Work on a website begins with registering a domain name and ends with checking the quality of the website, which is completely ready to be filled with content.

When using this guide to create a functioning website, it is recommended to document the actions performed in the companion Planner #2 (Website Development Planner).

The book contains many illustrations in the form of real screenshots with detailed comments.

The book is intended for people who do not have special technical training and do not have experience in creating websites.

The book is addressed to readers focused on creating a website independently or wanting to feel more confident when interacting with professional website developers. Also, this book can be helpful for students and those who want to start working in the Internet business.

Table of Contents

Foreword..10

1. Preparatory Stage...13

   Stage Tasks..13

   1.1. Registering a Domain Name for Your Website...13

      1.1.1. How to Choose a Domain Name Registrar Company.............................13

      1.1.2. How to Register a Domain Name...14

   1.2. Preparing Hosting for the Site...16

      1.2.1. Choosing a Hosting Company..16

      1.2.2. Registering an Account and Purchasing Hosting...................................17

      1.2.3. First Steps in the cPanel Console...19

   1.3. Domain Delegation..22

      1.3.1. How to Find Out Nameserver Names...22

      1.3.2. How to Use Nameserver Names...23

   1.4. Domain Checks...24

      1.4.1. How to Check Domain Delegation...24

      1.4.2. How to Check Domain Delegation Using the Ping Command.................24

      1.4.3. How to Check Domain Delegation in Browser..25

      1.4.4. How to Check Server Operation Using a Text File.................................26

   1.5. DNS Records..27

      1.5.1. Domain Zone and Its Records...27

      1.5.2. Inspecting Zone Records and Adding a CNAME Record.........................28

   1.6. Installing and Setting Up an SSL Certificate...29

      1.6.1. Checking SSL Certificate Status..29

      1.6.2. Activating an SSL Certificate Connection..30

      1.6.3. Actions After Connecting the SSL Certificate.......................................31

   1.7. System File .htaccess..33

   1.8. Website Database..34

      1.8.1. Creating a Database for the Website..34

      1.8.2. Creating a Database User Account...35

      1.8.3. Granting the Database User the Necessary Privileges.............................36

   Stage Results..39

2. Installing WordPress..41

  Stage Tasks...41

  2.1. Getting WordPress onto the Server...42

    2.1.1. Copying WordPress System to the Server........................42

    2.1.2. Unpacking WordPress System Files on the Server............43

  2.2. Preparing to Install WordPress...45

    2.2.1. The Last Step Before Installing WordPress.....................45

    2.2.2. Preparing the WordPress Configuration File....................45

  2.3. WordPress Installation...47

    2.3.1. Things to Have on Hand When Installing WordPress......47

    2.3.2. Running the WordPress Installer.....................................48

    2.3.3. First Login to the WordPress System on the Website......50

  2.4. First Look at the WordPress Interface.....................................51

    2.4.1. Important WordPress Interface Features..........................51

    2.4.2. WordPress Main Menu and Pages...................................52

    2.4.3. WordPress Interface Blocks and Work Areas..................55

  2.5. Initial WordPress Settings..57

    2.5.1. Where are the Settings Located?.....................................57

    2.5.2. Home Page and Other Reading Settings.........................58

    2.5.3. Settings That Affect Each Post.......................................59

  2.6. Checking the Website Health..62

    2.6.1. What Is Website Health, and What Needs to Be Done Now............62

    2.6.2. Removing Unused and Inactive Plugins...........................63

    2.6.3. Removing Inactive Themes...64

    2.6.4. Rechecking Website Health and Further Actions.............65

    2.6.5. Complete technical information about the website............66

    2.6.6. First Test Using Core Web Vitals...................................66

  Stage Results..70

3. Configuring the WordPress Website...71

  Stage tasks...71

  3.1. Editing the Administrator Account...72

  3.2. Modifying the .htaccess File..73

  3.3. Installing and Configuring Security Plugins............................75

    3.3.1. Installing the Multipurpose Plugin for Website Protection............75

    3.3.2. Setting Up the AIO WP Security Plugin.........................77

3.3.3. Disabling and Re-enabling the AIO WP Security plugin..................87

3.3.4. Plugin for Additional Protection Using a Firewall......................89

3.3.5. Additional WordPress File Verification Plugin...........................92

3.4. Closing the Website to Visitors..93

3.5. Installing and Configuring Performance Plugins..............................96

3.5.1. Backend Caching Plugin..96

3.5.2. Frontend Caching Plugin...98

3.5.3. Additional Plugins to Increase Website Performance.................100

3.6. Installing and Configuring SEO Plugins...101

3.6.1. Choosing and Installing an SEO Plugin.....................................101

3.6.2. How to Install the Extended Version of the Plugin....................102

3.6.3. SEO Plugin Setup..103

3.7. Installing Other Recommended Plugins..105

Stage Results...108

4. Customizing the Appearance of the WordPress Website.....................109

Stage Tasks...109

4.1. Classic WordPress Themes vs Block Themes.................................110

4.2. Choosing a WordPress Theme..112

4.2.1. Difficulties in Choosing a Theme..112

4.2.2. Sequence and Criteria for Choosing a Theme............................112

4.2.3. Preliminary Check of Selected Themes......................................114

4.3. Installing the Theme...117

4.3.1. The Truth About Using Themes on Desktop and Mobile...........117

4.3.2. Themes' Safety..118

4.3.3. How to Install a Theme...118

4.4. Creating the Child Theme...121

4.4.1. Why Do You Need a Child Theme?...121

4.4.2. The Easy Way to Create a Child Theme.....................................121

4.5. Setting Up the Theme...123

4.5.1. Where to Start Customizing the Theme......................................123

4.5.2. Where are Theme Settings?...124

4.5.3. Setting General Layout Options...126

4.5.4. Header and Footer Customization..130

4.5.5. Customizing Colors and Fonts...138

4.5.6. More About Theme Settings..142

4.6. Customizing the Theme with CSS File...143

    4.6.1. CSS Capabilities for a WordPress Site....................................143

    4.6.2. CSS Usage Examples...144

        4.6.2.1. Hiding Page Elements..144

        4.6.2.2. Changing the Appearance of Page Elements.....................145

        4.6.2.3. Changing the Appearance of Various Blocks.....................146

        4.6.2.4. Links in the Form of Buttons.....................................147

4.7. Classic Theme Usage..148

    4.7.1. Installing the Classic Theme..148

    4.7.2. Customizing the Classic Theme...149

    4.7.3. Additional Widget Capabilities..151

4.8. Checking Website Look...153

    4.8.1. Why is an Intermediate Check Needed and Where to Start?........153

    4.8.2. Visual Check Sequence...154

    4.8.3. What Needs to Be Done Later...154

  Stage Results..156

5. Structuring the WordPress Website..157

  Stage Tasks..157

5.1. Internal Structure of the Website...158

    5.1.1. Internal Structure of the Website and Its Appearance..............158

    5.1.2. What are Taxonomies..158

5.2. Creating Categories...160

    5.2.1. Number and Nesting of Categories....................................160

    5.2.2. The Importance of Correctly Linking Posts to Categories..........163

    5.2.3. How to Create Categories Correctly...................................163

    5.2.4. SEO for Categories..165

5.3. Creating Tags...165

    5.3.1. Differences Between Tags and Categories............................165

    5.3.2. How to Create Tags Correctly..167

    5.3.3. Attaching Tags to Posts and Their Place on the Website............169

    5.3.4. SEO for Tags..169

5.4. Adding Required Pages..170

    5.4.1. About Using Pages..170

    5.4.2. "About" Page...171

    5.4.3. "Privacy Policy" Page..172

5.4.4. "Terms and Conditions" Page..172

5.4.5. "Contacts" page...173

5.4.6. Additional Tips by Pages..173

5.5. Setting Up Menus..174

5.5.1. What are Menus and How to Use Them...174

5.5.2. Main Menu...176

5.5.3. Mobile Menu and Secondary Menu..176

5.5.4. Footer Menu..177

5.5.5. Social Menu..178

5.6. Checking the Visual Structure of the Site...180

5.6.1. Why and How to Check Pages of Various Types.....................................180

5.6.2. Testing Menus and Checking Layouts...180

5.6.2. Checklist for Final Inspection...181

Stage Results..182

Afterword...183

List of Illustrations...185

Foreword

Dear Reader!

This is the second book in the "Build and Monetize Your Own WordPress Website" series.

This book is about how to practically create your own website. There is nothing superfluous in it.

There are no descriptions of all the themes or plugins that the author liked, only the necessary minimum is indicated from which you can start working. There are no long stories here about how each problem can be solved in dozens of different ways.

There are no general guidelines or verbose instructions here, everything is shown with real examples showing real actions, so that after solving specific problems you will not have any ambiguities or questions about what specific actions need to be performed.

The book contains all the necessary information. Here you will find absolutely precise instructions. With these instructions you will take the first practical steps on the shortest path to your own website.

Everything is done clearly, simply, and clearly. There is nothing here that distracts from the main task. There is always one correct and short path, and we follow it.

The main task and sole purpose of this book is to guide you through the entire process of creating a website. All this is done using a real example. This example is a site that will be created before your eyes. You will see and understand everything you learn.

This book is aimed at getting the results you need with guaranteed quality.

The mission of this book is to teach beginners how to quickly and easily create technically high-quality websites. Such sites that will have an objectively confirmed level of quality, and not just please with their appearance. A website that works well and is simple in design is always much better than the most beautiful website that works poorly.

In this book you will find practical answers to more than 100 practical questions on 30 separate, very important tasks, without which it is impossible to create a website.

Each question is considered as a procedure for performing practical actions to solve a specific problem. Completing each of these steps will bring you one step closer to creating your own website. Each step will give you new knowledge and new skills.

Here's what you'll do to create your own website and be able to do in the future for yourself or for your clients.

1. You will create an account on the registrar's website and register your own domain name, connect security services to your account and activate additional protection for your account to perform important actions.

2. You will register an account with the hosting company, select the plan that suits you, activate it and check the initial settings.

3. You will connect the domain name to your server on the host and test domain delegation in various ways, including using a test file.

4. You will check and clarify the DNS settings for your domain name on the hosting server.

5. You will receive and connect an SSL certificate and check access to your site via the https protocol.

6. You will create the database that you will need to install and run WordPress.

7. You will create a database user account and grant this user all necessary permissions.

8. You will download the WordPress distribution kit from the official website, unpack it and place it in the desired folder.

9. You will prepare WordPress for installation, complete the installation, and test access and functionality of your new site.

10. You will close your site from visitors and search engines, leaving it visible only to yourself until the moment when it is ready for the official launch.

11. You will complete the initial settings of WordPress for all modes of its use and operation.

12. You will become familiar with the WordPress interface and customize it according to your needs and preferences.

13. You will check the health of the site and make sure it is ready for real work.

14. You will install and configure the plugins that are needed to ensure the security of your site.

15. You will review and configure WordPress user accounts for your site.

16. You will review and configure the reading and writing settings for your site's posts.

17. You will review and adjust the permalink format for future posts.

18. You will install and configure plugins that will provide your site with high performance.

19. You will install and configure SEO plugins that will ensure your site is treated well by search engines.

20. You will install and configure auxiliary plugins that will be required to solve various problems during the operation of the site.

21. You will select and install a theme that suits your needs and goals.

22. You will create a child theme based on the chosen theme, host it on the server and connect it to your site.

23. You will customize the appearance of your site using theme settings and using your own styles for individual elements and blocks.

24. You will check the appearance of different parts of your site and adjust it if necessary using theme settings and custom styles.

25. You will become familiar with the internal structure of the site and understand the relationship of all its components.

26. You will create and review the categories in which your posts will be published.

27. You will create and test tags that will serve as navigational elements for future site visitors.

28. You will create and provide content to the pages of the site that are considered necessary and mandatory.

29. You will create and configure a menu system for your website and test its operation.

30. You will set up the home page of your site and test its operation.

When you've done all this, you'll have a fully functional, carefully configured website, ready to host real content.

To ensure that all of the above work brings you maximum benefit, I strongly recommend that you use a specialized Planner #2 (Website Development Planner).

If you do not feel confident enough, I recommend that before starting work on a real website, you carefully read the book "WordPress Website Building 101", if you have not already read it, and use the Planner #1 that accompanies it (Website Concept Planner).

Author.

1

Preparatory Stage

Stage Tasks

This chapter covers all the work from the moment of registering a domain name until you are completely ready to install and initially configure the *Content Management System*.

In our case, this will, of course, be *CMS WordPress*.

The very first practical stage begins with registering a domain name. I hope you have already chosen a domain name for your project?

If you still have doubts, here are three simple practical tips.

Firstly, research domain zones on the *Internet Assigned Numbers Authority* website (*https://iana.org*) and select a zone that suits you.

Secondly, make a shortlist of potential domain names.

Thirdly, check the options you came up with on the registrar's website for uniqueness and determine the potential resale value.

As a result, you will be able to choose a domain name that suits your project and will be of independent value.

The information that you will receive at this stage is absolutely universal and will be useful to you for working with any companies providing domain name registration and hosting services. The main thing is that the hosting provides the *cPanel* system for website management. We will work with this system, and I strongly recommend that you focus on it.

We will study all the questions using the example of our project's main training website, available at *https://buildown.site*. Some additional examples will be shown on the project's auxiliary website at *https://buildown.website*.

1.1. Registering a Domain Name for Your Website

1.1.1. How to Choose a Domain Name Registrar Company

Very often, inexperienced website owners register domain names with a hosting company on whose servers they plan to host their websites. Many hosting companies have made free domain name registration part of their marketing policy. Typically, the period for such registration is one year.

If you have no experience, then this solution, of course, will seem tempting and profitable to you. Discounted hosting, free domain name, and all this - in one place, without unnecessary hassle.

The extra hassle starts later. When it turns out that the hosting is not as good as expected and you decide to change it.

For example, it turns out that there is a moratorium on domain name transfers for a period of one year, during which you must use hosting services. In this case, if an emergency site transfer is necessary, there is even a risk of losing the domain name.

You need to understand that for hosting companies, registering and maintaining domain names is not their main business, so you will have to transfer the site to another server along with the domain name.

This means you'll have to deal with transferring your domain name, which isn't always easy to do. And only after transferring the domain name will you be able to place your website under this name on the new host.

And, finally, one more trifle that cannot be avoided: with this transfer option, along with the domain name, your site will inevitably become unavailable for some time. It will simply stop working for anywhere from a few minutes to 3 days.

I recommend that you use the services of a specialized company - a domain name registrar to register a domain name. Such companies often provide hosting services, and this can be very convenient. But if you decide to change the hosting company, then you will not have any problems in this case.

You can change hosts as often as you like. In this case, the domain name will continue to be supported by the registrar and will not need to be transferred anywhere.

In addition, it will be possible to transfer a website from one host to another so that it will always be available and visible to the whole world. This is very easy to do and in the second part of the course you will learn how to do it.

And finally, a specialized domain name registrar company offers many very useful services related to domain names. Hosting companies simply do not provide such services.

The domain names for this book's project sites (and some of my other projects) are registered with *GoDaddy*. I have been using their services for many years. This is probably the largest and most reliable domain name registrar in the world and I can recommend it to you. Keep in mind that large domain name registrars also offer hosting services and have excellent capabilities for this.

A short summary of what they said looks something like this.

If you register a domain name with a large registrar company, then purchasing hosting from the same company will not cause you problems, and if you eventually want to switch to hosting from another provider, then you simply will not have to transfer the domain name, it will remain with the company - registrar

If you decide to purchase both of these services from a company that specializes in hosting and is not a large registrar, then you will almost inevitably have problems transferring your domain name in the future when you change hosting providers.

The choice is yours, but at the initial stage it is important to register a domain name with a reliable company.

There is nothing complicated in the registration process itself. This is similar to any online purchase.

1.1.2. How to Register a Domain Name

We'll look at registering a domain name using *GoDaddy* (*https://godaddy.com*).

Create an account on the company's website, save the email address and password you used, as well as the customer number that will be used as a login, and a *PIN* code that you may need to use when communicating with customer service if problems arise. I have never needed this code once in 15 years of working with this company. Be sure to enable two-factor authentication using your mobile phone number.

The registration process is very simple (Figure 1-1). You enter the domain name you are interested in and the registrar will tell you if it is available and how much it costs to register it.

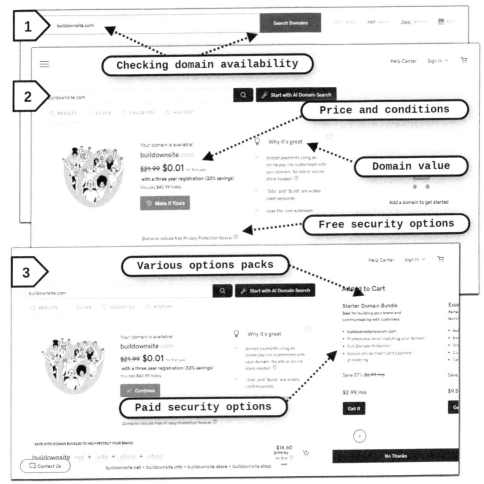

Figure 1-1. Choosing and Registering a Domain Name.

Keep in mind that domain names that are already registered can sell for very high prices. Domain names that are considered premium can also be expensive. But that doesn't mean you can't get a good domain name for the standard price, and even with a big discount for the first year of registration.

If you have serious plans, then a very reasonable option is to register a domain name for at least two years. With such registration, you can get a good discount on a domain name and additional services. In addition, domain names registered for more than a year are believed to be more popular with search engines.

A basic security package that allows you to hide your personal information can be provided free of charge. It is highly recommended to purchase additional full domain name protection. It doesn't cost much, and skimping on security can cost you significantly more expensive problems down the road. Don't skimp on safety!

After you place and pay for your order, the domain name becomes available to you immediately. You can verify this if you enter your domain name into the address bar of your browser and press *Enter*. You will see that your domain name exists and that the whole world is eagerly waiting for your website to appear.

This page is automatically displayed by the registrar company. You will see that your domain name exists, that the connection to it uses the insecure *HTTP* protocol, and that you do not yet have a website.

We will look for solutions to all these problems on the website of the hosting company.

1.2. Preparing Hosting for the Site

1.2.1. Choosing a Hosting Company

In the first book in the series, the issue of choosing a hosting company was discussed in some detail. You can return to this book if necessary to remember the most important details of this process.

The sites of the project, which includes this book, have been on the servers of different hosting companies. This was necessary in order to compare the quality of hosting services and the quality of work of the same sites at slightly different monetary costs.

Essentially, an experiment was conducted on the same ready-to-use, fairly simple sites. It took about six months, during which the functioning of the sites was tested on 12 servers of various hosting companies.

As a result of the work performed, it was possible to establish that in recent years the quality of technical services provided by various hosting companies has hardly varied. This is due to the reduction in cost of modern servers using *SSD* drives, and a sharp increase in the quality and capacity of data transmission channels and telecommunications equipment.

Therefore, in most cases, looking for a "faster" hoster does not make much sense. But, of course, it is necessary to check the quality of services. The level of comfort that customer service can provide is also important. This is a very individual question, and it needs to be resolved in each case, based on your ideas about interaction.

As a result, it was decided to host the sites of this project on *GoDaddy* servers. We will not compare them with servers from other companies. Let us note the reasons why these servers were considered suitable for this project.

1. This company is the largest domain name registrar. This means that it has a large and highly reliable network of servers and storage, guaranteed to provide high-quality and uninterrupted operation.
2. The availability of high-quality hosting services and domain name registration in one company simultaneously ensures a sufficient level of hosting quality and site name security.
3. The company provides very competitive tariff plans at affordable prices. Clients do not have to overpay for reliability and security.
4. The company has a huge number of server configurations provided. Among these configurations there are the most popular and popular combinations of the *Linux* operating system on the market, the *cPanel* user console, and support for the *WordPress CMS*.

This is exactly what was needed for this project.

In addition, the company provides many ready-made service packages for the further development of websites for various purposes.

If you want company reliability and development prospects, then you can order both domain registration and hosting from *GoDaddy*. Their tariff plans are very attractive, especially in the "Web Hosting" section (Figure 1-2). If you only have one website, then the "Standard" plan is suitable for you. If there are several sites, then any of the following options will be suitable - your choice. Another big advantage of this company is a very flexible payment system, with terms from one month to three years.

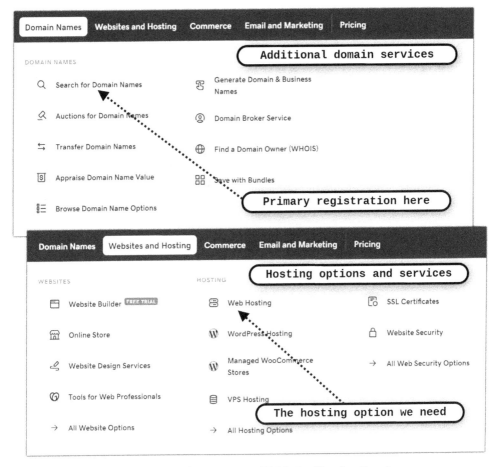

Figure 1-2. Domain Names and Website Hosting Services.

Of course, choosing a hosting company for your project is your prerogative.

The project's information website publishes current information about hosting companies; you can always find this information at ***https://buildownsite.com/tag/hosting/***.

1.2.2. Registering an Account and Purchasing Hosting

The process of registering an account and purchasing services is standard, everything happens as usual. Pay attention to the geographic location of the servers (if the hosting company provides a choice) and choose the one that is closer to your target audience if you intend to target a local audience.

An important point: be sure to indicate the domain name that you have already registered when placing an order for hosting services! And be sure to indicate that you are using an existing domain name!

Once you have access to the host, we will take all necessary steps to ensure that the domain name you registered with the registrar company is associated with your host.

Immediately after registration and payment you will receive confirmation that your server is ready for use.

To check, you can simply open your *cPanel* hosting management console. This can usually be done by clicking on an easily recognizable icon or a special link (Figure 1-3).

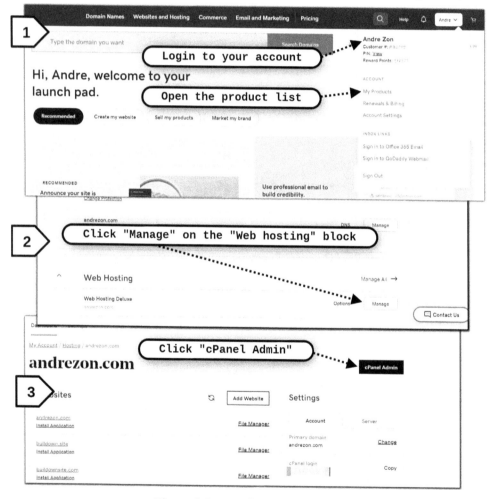

Figure 1-3. cPanel Access Method.

Once you launch the *cPanel* console, you do not need to perform any special actions. You have registered an account, paid for hosting services, gained access to the server and successfully launched the *cPanel* console.

You can be absolutely sure that your hosting issue has been successfully resolved and you can continue working. There is no need to perform any special actions with the *cPanel* console. In the future, you can customize the appearance of its interface to your liking - choose a design theme, swap windows with tools and minimize those that you do not plan to use.

Now you just need to get used to it a little (Figure 1-4).

1.2.3. First Steps in the cPanel Console

Your main tool in this console is the *File Manager* application. Launch it and make sure that you see the directory tree on the left side of the window and the contents of the current directory or folder on the right side.

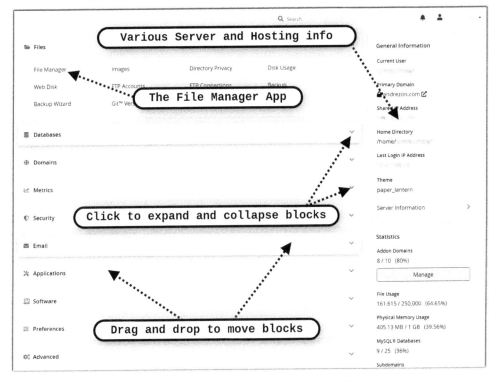

Figure 1-4. The cPanel Interface and access to the File Manager app.

Very important! When you've just launched the *File Manager* application, you can see on both the left and right sides of the window the root directory of your virtual web server. There are many directories in it that you will never need to open, and some that you shouldn't open (Figure 1-5).

Among the directories you see, only one is designed to house all the resources on your site. Only one!

Immediately after launching the *File Manager* application, you will see this directory on the right side of the window with a globe icon and the name *public_html*. The right side of the window is working, and its contents are not permanent. Here, the contents of directories are opened, and basic actions with directories and files are performed.

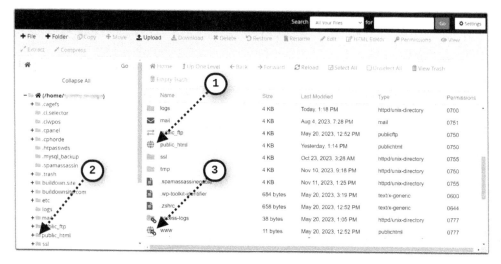

Figure 1-5. Three ways to access the root directory of the website.

On the left side of the window, where the webserver directories are presented as a tree, the contents never change. Here, the directory with the content of your site, of course, is also called *public_html*.

If you look closely at the right side of the window, at the very bottom you will see another line with a globe icon and chain links, which is called *www* and in the *"Type"* column is designated as *"public_html"*.

This is just another line that, when double-clicked, opens the same root directory of your site (get used to not confusing it with the root directory of your part of the web server!).

This is just another, third way to open the folder with all your site data. This folder has nothing to do with the third-level domain that begins with *"www"*. It just has such an archaic and confusing designation.

Let's assume that this is just a tribute to some tradition.

A note for the future. When we look at creating multiple sites on one host, you will see that each site will also only have one directory.

For now, all you need is the *public_html* folder. I have my personal website information here, and the project website and training website we are creating are hosted on additional domains (Figure 1-6).

Just ignore it for now.

Working with additional domains makes it easy to add new sites on the same host. This is a very useful feature and you will probably need it in the future. Now you just saw that it exists, and in the final sessions later you will learn more about it.

Find the *public_html* folder with the globe image and double-click it as usual. You will see a subfolder in this folder called *cgi-bin* and nothing else. You are unlikely to need this subfolder in the future, and you can simply delete it.

Now you need to perform a small but very important action (Figure 1-7).

At the top of the *File Manager* interface, click on the *Preferences* icon to open a dialog box. Check if the *Show Hidden Files (dotfiles)* checkbox is active.

If it is active, click *Cancel* or simply close the dialog.

If the checkbox is inactive, activate it and click the *Save* button.

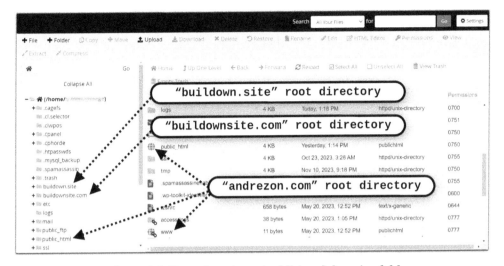

Figure 1-6. Root domain and additional domains folders.

Now you will see all the files, including hidden ones, among which there is one very important file. We're talking about a *.htaccess* file whose name starts with a dot. We will see and edit this file many more times.

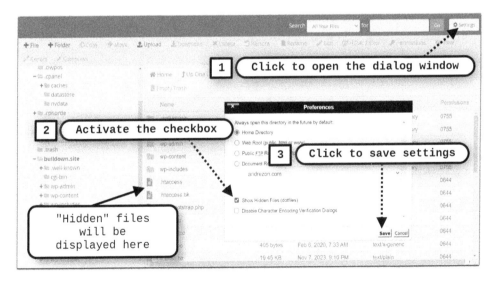

Figure 1-7. Changing File Manager preferences to display hidden files.

Everything works as it should.

You can close File Manager, you will need it for real work after successfully binding the domain to the host.

We will now start linking the domain to your future website.

1.3. Domain Delegation

1.3.1. How to Find Out Nameserver Names

So, the first steps have been taken. We have a domain name that is registered and secured. We have a host on which our site will run. We need to associate a domain name with a host.

If you purchased hosting services from the company that registered the domain name for you, the domain name will be linked to hosting automatically. In this case, you do not need to perform any additional actions, and you can go straight to section *1.4. Domain Checks*.

If you registered a domain name and purchased hosting services from different companies, then you will need to follow a few simple steps.

As you already understand, the registrar ensures that the registered domain is connected to the worldwide *DNS* system. After registering the domain, we were convinced of this: our domain name opens a page that was automatically generated by the registrar. This page is located on the registrar host.

We must give the registrar the names of our host's name servers so that the worldwide *DNS* system directs all requests related to our domain to our host, to the same folder on the server that we checked using the *File Manager* component of the *cPanel* console.

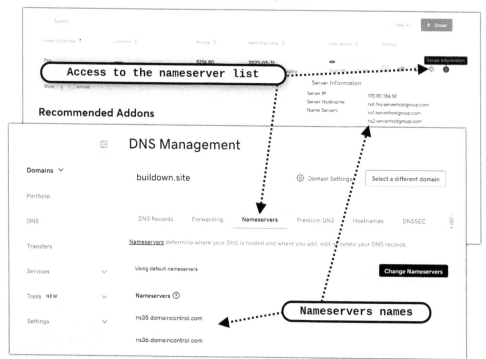

Figure 1-8. Access to nameserver data - various options exist.

Here's what we need to do.

Log in to your account on the hosting site. In the line that contains the already familiar icon for going to the *cPanel* console, there is an icon that, when clicked, displays hosting information. Some hosters display it in a special block of information about the server (Figure 1-8).

This is the information we need. Identify nameserver names. Write them down on a piece of paper or copy them into a text editor, or immediately enter them into special fields in the Planner.

These names must be entered into the registrar's database using a special form. In the process of making changes, the registrar will definitely ask for confirmation of your actions, and if you have already activated two-factor authentication, it will ask you to enter a code that will be sent to your phone number via *SMS*. Don't worry, you're doing everything right. If your hosting company has not made sure that nameserver names are easy to find (highly unlikely), contact technical support.

1.3.2. How to Use Nameserver Names

Open your account on the registrar's website and go to the page with a list of your products. In the line with the domain name, click on "*DNS*".

In the window that opens, find the block with the names of name servers and click the "*Change*" button. After confirmation, you will see a form consisting of two fields. If your hosting uses three nameservers, click the "*Add Nameserver*" button, and there will be three fields.

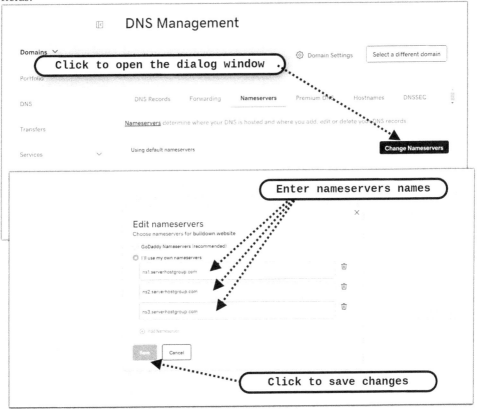

Figure 1-9. Changing nameservers names - an option.

Enter the names of the nameservers in these fields, without breaking their sequence - first the first name, then the second, and finally the third.

Click on the *"Save"* button and complete any confirmations that the registrar may request.

After this, you do not need to perform any actions with the domain name on the registrar's website.

If you ever need to change hosting company, the steps to link your domain name to the new host will be exactly the same.

The registrar will not be offended by you, and nothing bad will happen to your domain name. This is a service that you purchased from the registrar along with the protection package, and he will provide this service to you regardless of what hosting you use.

This completes the binding of the domain name to the host.

You don't need to do anything else on the registrar's website.

Now we just have to wait. In the next step you will learn how to do it correctly.

1.4. Domain Checks

1.4.1. How to Check Domain Delegation

Have you done everything right and you want to quickly make sure that your domain works and it will really become your website?

Be patient. You will not need to wait more than 72 hours. But in fact, everything usually happens much faster, sometimes within a few minutes.

I'll tell you a little secret. Once you register your domain name with *GoDaddy*, the 72 hour period begins immediately. This company certainly knows how to cut it short. That's why you saw a page under your domain name saying that something phenomenal will soon appear in its place.

Your domain was delegated and linked to *GoDaddy* servers shortly after registration. After changing nameservers, the global *DNS* system has a little less work to do in delegating your domain to the new host.

Therefore, you most likely will not need to wait more than a few hours.

1.4.2. How to Check Domain Delegation Using the Ping Command

The easiest way to test domain delegation is to launch a command terminal and enter the ping command with the domain name as a parameter. If you're on *Windows 11*, you need the *PowerShell* terminal that comes with it. Launch *PowerShell* and enter the command

```
ping domainname.zone
```

Here *domainname.zone* is the domain name you registered.

If you're on *MacOS*, launch the *Network Utility* app. Open the *Ping* tab, enter the domain name and number of packages in the form fields (from 4 to 10 is enough) and click the *Ping* button.

If the domain is not yet delegated, then the ping command simply will not be able to receive any response through the global *DNS* system, so you will receive a message that the domain was not found.

If the domain is successfully delegated, you will see the test results in the form of a message about the *IP* address of the server to which the domain is linked, and lines with test results using test data packets.

Each line will indicate the time it takes for the server to process the test packet. At the bottom of the message you will see general statistics and the average processing time for the test data packet.

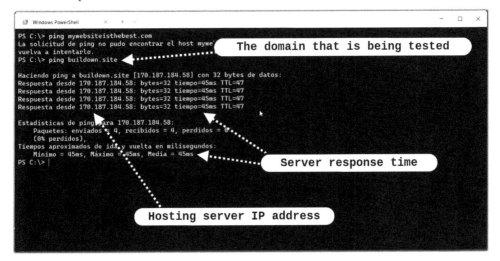

Figure 1-10. Check domain availability using the Windows console.

The faster the server response time, the better. The closer the test results are to each other, the more stable the server is. If the test packet processing time is the same for all attempts, then the server is very stable and your connection to it is working fine.

What time is considered good? This depends not only on the quality of the server, but also on the distance between this server and your computer. Within one continent, this time can be considered good if it is less than 50-60 *ms*. If it is 100-150 *ms*, then this is normal if your computer and server are on different continents.

This time can only be reduced by using *CDN* (*Content Delivery Networks*) systems, which allow you to place part of the website data on special servers located in different parts of the world. We will look at this topic in due course. For now, just remember this abbreviation.

So, running the *ping* command showed that the domain was successfully delegated.

1.4.3. How to Check Domain Delegation in Browser

Please be aware that there may be a delay in the domain being available in the browser.

This is because the browser and the *ping* command deal with different routes that connect your computer and your site's host.

To check, type the domain name in the address bar of the browser and press *Enter*. We will see a gray page with huge numbers that make up the 404 code. What does this mean?

Firstly, our domain is accessible, otherwise we would see a completely different page, something like this.

Secondly, this is not the same page from the registrar company that we saw after registering the domain. This is another page. This means that our new host is showing it to us.

Thirdly, code 404 is the standard response from the web server if the requested document is not available on the host. By default, this is a file called *index.html*, although other options are possible. We have a completely empty directory there, and there is nothing in it at all. That's why we see code like this.

Now we will create a special verification file on the host, in the directory of the future site. With its help, we will finally make sure that the domain name leads to where we need it - to the directory of the future site on the host.

1.4.4. How to Check Server Operation Using a Text File

Log in to your hosting account and open your *cPanel* console. Launch *File Manager* and enter the site's root folder. Click on the create a new file icon. In our case, let it be a regular text file, which we will call *test.txt*.

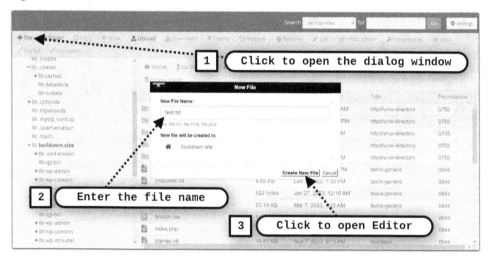

Figure 1-11. Creating a text file in the website's root directory.

Open the created file for editing, type some verification text in it and save the file.

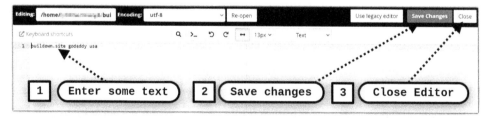

Figure 1-12. Editing and saving a text file with the File Manager.

Now enter the full address of the page in the address bar of the browser, which contains the domain name and the name of the created text file (e.g., ***http://buildown.site/test.txt***).

The browser will display the text string that we wrote in the test file.

So, it's not a website yet, but this is definitely where it will be. This place is in your new reality, and you need to feel at home here. We need to start settling into the new space.

Let's start by checking and clarifying some information related to the *DNS* records of our domain.

1.5. DNS Records

1.5.1. Domain Zone and Its Records

Please be aware that the hosting company may limit the capabilities of the zone editor using *cPanel* if other tools are provided. This is exactly what *GoDaddy* does because it is also a registrar company. Other companies specializing in hosting and not primary registrars provide more options in *cPanel* because they do not have direct access to domain data. This refers to the situation when the hosting company is not the registrar of your domain.

If you are hosting with a large registrar such as *GoDaddy*, you need to go to the "*My Products*" page you already know, go to the *DNS* edit page for the required domain, and ensure no action is needed on it. The system configures everything automatically, and it's best not to touch anything here (Figure 1-13).

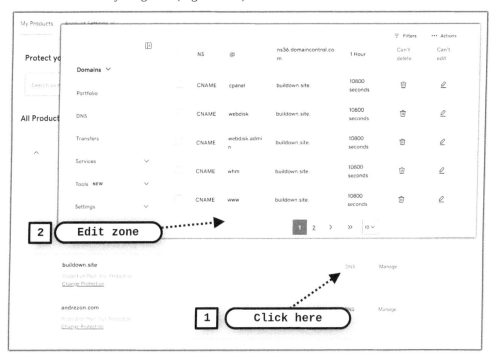

Figure 1-13. Invoking the domain zone record settings page.

If you use the services of an independent host, find the *Domains* block in the *cPanel* interface and in this block - the Zone Editor application. Launch this application.

You will see a table with a row with your domain name. I have a lot of domains here, so a lot of lines. I click the "*Manage*" button in the line with the domain name.

The application window displays a list of "domain zone" records (Figure 1-14).

Here's a short explanation about this list. It is stored in a special file, which is often called a "zone file", or a "domain zone file." This file is precisely the link between the global *DNS* system and your domain.

The number of entries in this file may vary, and each entry is of a type. The *Type A* record is the most required; it is the one that links your domain name to the server address. The remaining entries have different purposes, and we will not study them. This is a topic for a separate discussion, and this knowledge is only needed by system administrators and technical specialists.

Our task now is very easy. We need to add one record of type *CNAME*.

1.5.2. Inspecting Zone Records and Adding a CNAME Record

We need to look at the list and determine if there is a *CNAME* record in the list whose *Name* field contains a domain name with the prefix "*www*."

My domain already has such an entry, but I'll show you how to add it if it doesn't exist. As you can see, it's easy to do. Enter exactly the same information as in the line my domain already has; just change the domain name to yours. The domain name with the prefix "*www*," located in the *Name* field, must contain a dot at the end without a space before it.

After filling in all the fields of the line to be filled in, click the *Save Record* button. Done!

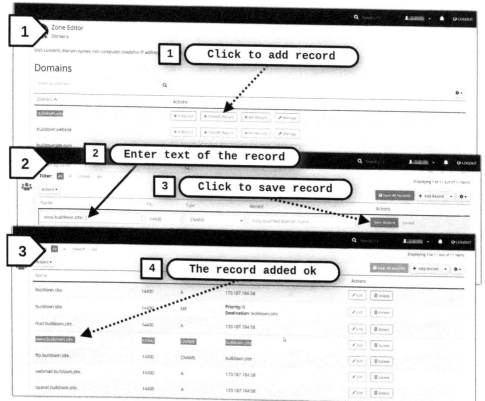

Figure 1-14. Invoking the Zone Editor in cPanel.

Now, domain names with and without the prefix "*www*" are synonymous.

After installing *WordPress* and as part of the process of linking your site to search engines, we will take additional steps that will ultimately convince search engines that the main version of all pages on your site does not contain the "*www*" prefix and pages with such a prefix are not duplicates.

In the future, you may still need the *DNS* zone editor to add *TXT* records to place verification codes in them, for example, from *Google Search Console*. But this is still in the future. Now, we no longer need the zone editor.

Click the "*Save All Records*" button and return to the *cPanel* home page.

Let's continue preparations for creating the site. A simple but crucial step awaits us - connecting an *SSL* certificate to ensure the website operates using the secure https protocol.

1.6. Installing and Setting Up an SSL Certificate

1.6.1. Checking SSL Certificate Status

Honestly, everything here should work automatically. But any automation can malfunction, so at critical moments, it requires human intervention.

Installing an *SSL* certificate is one such thing.

Since we are connecting a free certificate, it should be installed automatically when creating an account.

But we will consider the case when we associate a domain name registered with another company to a host. When creating an account with a hosting company, this name was not yet linked to the host; we linked it later.

Therefore, the hosting robot, which immediately after registering an account was supposed to install an *SSL* certificate for our domain, simply could not detect our domain, which had not yet been delegated to the new host by that time.

It is possible that while we were busy linking the domain name and checking the *DNS* zone records, the robot had already managed to re-check our domain, make sure that it was successfully delegated, and do everything needed to install the *SSL* certificate.

This is exactly what we will check now. If the robot has already done all the work, then we will simply make sure of this. If not, then we'll make a couple of mouse clicks and help the robot deal with it.

On the main *cPanel* screen, find the *Security* block and launch the "*SSL/TSL Status*" application. You will see a page with a table that will have only two columns - "*Domain*" and "*Certificate Status*" (Figure 1-15).

You might be surprised to learn that there are multiple versions of your domain. Or rather, third-level domains. This is normal.

In each row of the table, in the "*Certificate Status*" column, there should be an icon with a green closed padlock and the inscription "*AutoSSL Domain Validated*." This means that the certificate has been successfully installed, is active, and the site can operate using the https protocol.

If you see an icon with a red open padlock and the inscription "*AutoSSL Domain Not Validated*" in the lines related to your domain, then your intervention is required.

You need to activate the extraordinary launch of the *SSL* automatic connection program.

I'll show you how to perform it.

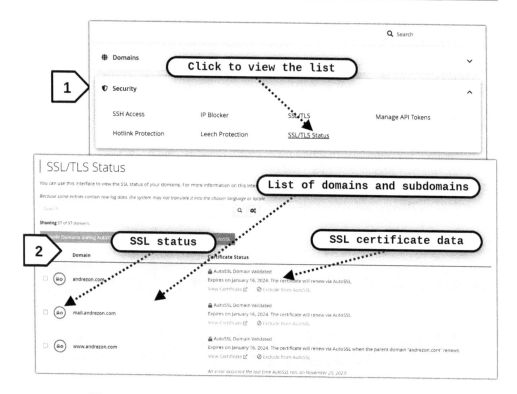

Figure 1-15. List of website versions and installed SSL certificates.

1.6.2. Activating an SSL Certificate Connection

You need to activate the checkbox next to the name of the second-level domain, which does not have any prefixes. This domain is the root of all others, so whatever happens to it will immediately occur to third-level domains. Therefore, there is no need to activate any more checkboxes.

Then, above the table, find the "*Run AutoSSL*" button and click it once (Figure 1-16). After a short period of time, all the locks will close and turn green, and the words "*AutoSSL Domain Validated*" will appear next to them.

This usually takes a few seconds or a few minutes. You have done everything correctly, and after the successful completion of *SSL* certificate activation, your site is ready to operate using a secure protocol.

Please note that the right column of the table indicates the date of the next automatic renewal of the *SSL* certificate. On this day, you should return to this table and check if everything is in order. If necessary, if you see red pads here, do what we just talked about - activate the checkbox next to the domain name and click the "*Run AutoSSL*" button.

Events such as the failure of automatic renewal of a free *SSL* certificate are infrequent.

In my many years of experience working with dozens of domains, this happened only once. I learned about this quite quickly: real-time site traffic statistics began falling rapidly. After a couple of minutes, I found the problematic domain and clicked the "*Run AutoSSL*" button for it.

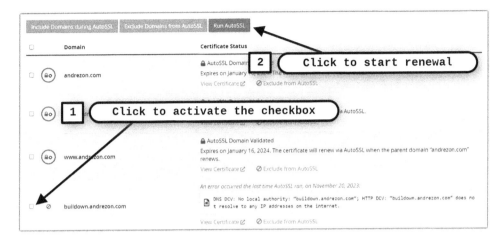

Figure 1-16. Forced activation of an SSL certificate.

Later I found out that this incident was related to updating the hosting servers, and a little later - that I was warned about this in a letter, which, for some reason, I did not read.

Always read emails from your registrar and your host!

And don't forget about important points that need to be controlled. Let me remind you that this is exactly why I created Planners.

1.6.3. Actions After Connecting the SSL Certificate

Let's return to our site.

After the certificates become active, we will check this fact using the browser.

Let's enter the full address of our test text file in the browser's address bar, but use the https protocol. As you can see, it opens without problems (Figure 1-17). The secure protocol works!

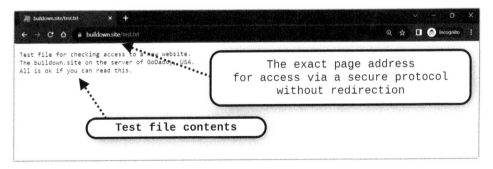

Figure 1-17. Checking access to a test file using a secure protocol.

We can look at the *SSL* certificate details and ensure everything is okay (Figure 1-18).

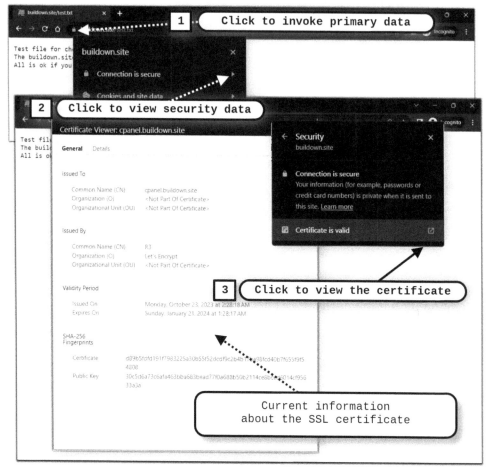

Figure 1-18. Browser window with information about the SSL certificate.

This is very good. And now, to make it clear what we will do in the next step, we will repeat opening the same text test file but using the usual *http* protocol. As you can see, our test file also opens, but the view of the browser address bar causes unpleasant thoughts. Our harmless test file with ordinary letters is flagged as an unsafe page!

But that's not all the trouble. If we leave everything as it is, then search engines will consider that site pages that open using the *http* protocol and site pages that are available using the *https* protocol are different pages because they have different addresses.

Therefore, search engines will crawl and index the same content twice - as different pages. After indexing, search engines will find that the same content is published on your site twice under different addresses, and this will be considered search spam. After this, the site, as you understand, will not be able to count on good positions in search results.

What needs to be done to prevent this from happening?

Very simple. You need to redirect all *http* requests to addresses that use the *https* protocol. This must be done in a way that is absolutely clear to search engines.

To do this, we will need to start working with the *.htaccess* file.

1.7. System File .htaccess

Do you remember what we already said about the *.htaccess* file being a hidden file? And that in the *File Manager* settings of the cPanel console, you need to activate a checkbox that controls their display in the list of files? And you already did it?

Very good. This means you are serious about success and are doing everything right. And you will not have problems working with such an important file as *.htaccess*.

Let's start by creating this file.

In the *cPanel* console, launch *File Manager* as usual, enter the site directory and click the *Create File* button. Specify a file name whose first character is a dot.

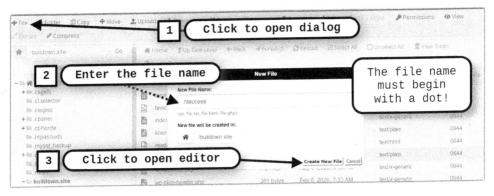

Figure 1-19. Creating the *.htaccess* file.

After creating the file, open it in edit mode and paste the following code into it.

```
# this domain use HTTPS only
<IfModule mod_rewrite.c>
RewriteEngine on
RewriteCond %{HTTPS} off
RewriteCond %{HTTP:X-Forwarded-Proto} !https
RewriteRule ^(.*)$ https://%{HTTP_HOST}%{REQUEST_URI} [L,R=301]
</IfModule>

# this domain should only be contacted in HTTPS for the next 12 months
<IfModule mod_headers.c>
Header set Strict-Transport-Security "max-age=31536000" env=HTTPS
</IfModule>
```

Save the file and close the editor. Now, check how the test file opens. Enter the full address of the test file in your browser to access it via the http protocol. The address will automatically switch to the https protocol (Figure 1-20).

The code we saved in the .htaccess file performs an operation known as a "*301 redirect*". When this operation is performed, in response to a request for any address, a new address is issued to which redirection is made, and the program that sent the request receives a special response code from our server.

This code is the number 301, which indicates a permanent redirect. If you make such a change of address, then search engines simply replace the old addresses in their databases with new ones.

In our case, there is no question of any change of addresses.

The code we just wrote in the *.htaccess* file accomplishes a critical task.

Search engines will remember your page addresses as safe from the very first visit. This happens because, on the very first visit, the search engine robot will immediately open a page addressed using the secure *https* protocol. There simply won't be any unsafe pages on the site.

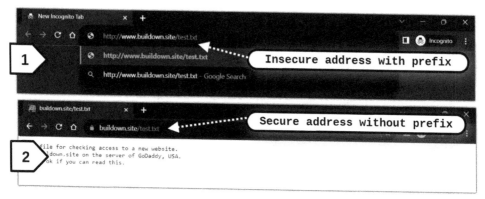

Figure 1-20. Checking redirection to access a test file via a secure protocol.

A little later, when preparing the finished site for opening, we will return to this issue and finally solve it with the help of another very important file.

At this stage, we have finished working with the domain, and it's time for us to begin solving the final task of the preparatory stage.

1.8. Website Database

1.8.1. Creating a Database for the Website

We've done almost all of the pre-installation work for *WordPress*.

All that remains is to create the database and user account.

The database is one of the main elements of the *WordPress* infrastructure. A database stores a lot of data. This is information related to the *WordPress* site and configuration, settings and status data for themes and plugins, and some of the site's content.

Without a database, *WordPress* cannot work.

The main type of database that *WordPress* works with is the *MySQL* database. These are the databases that are standardly used by the vast majority of hosters and websites. This is exactly the database we need to create.

A database user account is, as in many cases familiar to us, a login, password, and a list of authorities. This is very similar to a user account for some Internet service, isn't it?

Yes, that's right. Only the database server acts as a service and the *WordPress* system on which our site will run acts as its client.

However, the *WordPress installer*, for reasons related to hosting security, does not have the ability to create either databases or user accounts for them. This can only be done by the user of the hosting account. That is you.

Or me if we are talking about my account as it is now.

As a full-fledged user of the hosting of my future website, I will show you how it's done.

Create a database name, username, and password. Record them on paper or in a file so you don't lose them.

In the *cPanel* interface, find the *Databases* block and launch the *MySQL Databases* application in it.

In the page that opens, the top block is called *Create New Database* (Figure 1-21).

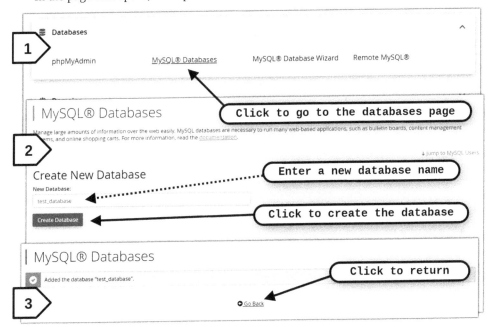

Figure 1-21. Creating a new database for the future site.

In the line, enter the name of your database and click the *Create Database* button. The database will be created immediately, and in a new window, you will see the message "Added the database...". Click the "*Go Back*" button on the right under this message, and you will be returned to the *MySQL Databases* page.

Now you need to create a user account.

1.8.2. Creating a Database User Account

Scroll down the page and find the "*MySQL Users*" block. In the *Username* line, enter the user name, and in the *Password* and *Password (Again)* lines - the password (Figure 1-22).

If you decide to use a password generator, you must be sure to save the offered password immediately. It is not stored anywhere, and you cannot spy on it later.

Ensure that the password strength indicator is green and that the password is rated as "strong" by the validator.

Click the "*Create User*" button. The account will be created immediately, and the browser window will automatically display a page with the message "*You have successfully created a MySQL user...*".

Click the "*Go Back*" button on the right under this message, and you will be returned to the *MySQL Databases* page.

Now, we have a database and a user account.

They exist separately from each other, and we now need to link the user account to the database.

In this case, the user (which means *WordPress*) must receive all the necessary permissions for operations with the database.

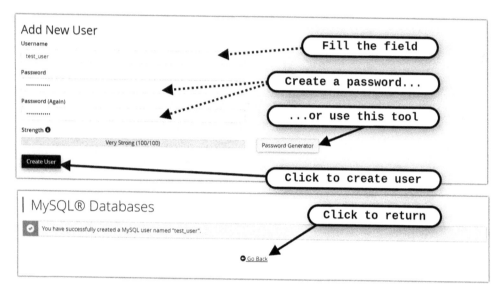

Figure 1-22. Creating a new database user for the future site.

1.8.3. Granting the Database User the Necessary Privileges

Scroll down the page and find the "*Add User to Database*" block (Figure 1-23).

From the *User* list, select the name of the created database user account, and from the *Database* list, select the name of the created database.

Click the "*Add*" button.

The "*Manage User Privileges*" page will open in the browser window. Activate the topmost checkbox "*ALL PRIVILEGES.*"

All checkboxes in the table will be activated automatically, and you no longer need to perform any actions with them. If you deactivate any checkbox, *WordPress* will not be able to work with your database.

Make sure that all checkboxes in the table are activated, and click the "*MakeChanges*" button.

The *Privilege Management* page will close automatically, and you will be returned to the *Database Management* page (Figure 1-24).

Copy and save the full *Database Name* and full *User Name* from the tables on this page in a text file or write in the Planner. These names and the password you saved will be required when installing *WordPress*.

No further database operations need to be performed. Return to the main page of your *cPanel* console.

Now, you will see another application that you will need in the future for backing up the site database and, possibly - but unlikely - for some other actions.

In the *Databases* block, the *phpMyAdmin* application is in first place. It is a very famous and well-reputed database application.

Launch this application.

You will see a list of databases on the left side of the window.

There are many of them here because I have a lot of sites on this host. This list also includes the database we just created (Figure 1-25).

If you click on its name, then on the right side of the window, we will see the message "*No tables found in database.*" This is entirely true - our database is completely empty.

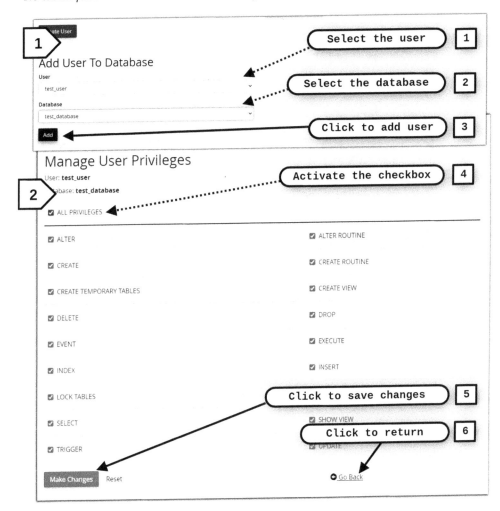

Figure 1-23. Granting privileges to the database user.

After installing *WordPress*, this picture will change.

We will learn and perform *WordPress* installation in the next part of the book.

And now, when we have wholly completed the first - preparatory - stage of work, the right moment has come to sum up and document all the completed actions in the Planner.

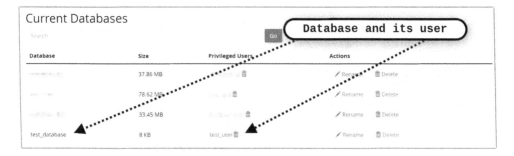

Figure 1-24. General information about databases and their users.

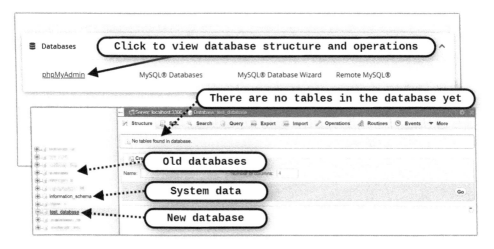

Figure 1-25. Interface to access database operations.

Stage Results

We have successfully completed all the preparatory phase work. It was a short but very, very important stage.

At the beginning of this stage, you had nothing but a domain name that you liked. That name was written down on a piece of paper next to the additional variants, right? Perhaps there are still very interesting domain name options that you like and may still be helpful in the future.

But you now have a domain name that has become more than a series of letters written on a piece of paper.

This name can now evoke an incredibly inspiring response from a browser that was previously just a window to the Internet for you and could show cool websites, play videos, make purchases, and read very interesting and useful publications.

Now, your web browser has become much more interesting: it can show a line of a test file that opens as a page of your real website, and at the same time - using your real, your own domain name.

But that's not all. You learned how to use the main *cPanel* console applications and create and edit files. You have made access to your website secure and created a database and a user account.

You have learned things that you may have never even heard of before. You are convinced that all this is not very scary and not very difficult.

It will be even more interesting further.

To ensure that everything works the first time, that information is not lost, and that you have complete control over everything that happens, you need to do one simple thing.

Record everything you have done at this stage in the Planner.

Do this always for all Planner pages at all subsequent stages of work. The day will come when this will save your project or provide you with an invaluable service in your work with a client for whom you, already an experienced website creator, will create another project.

Upon completion of each stage of work, I will remind you to fill out the Planner. I want to be sure that my efforts were not in vain and that everything is working out for you the way it should work out.

I have to be a pedant and a bit of a bore, especially when it comes to such vital things as future earnings. There are no small details here. Most likely, I am much older than you, and therefore, I have some reason and even right to be a grump.

But I really want you to succeed! And for this, you need the main thing. The main thing is a high-quality result, that is, a well-made website.

The next step towards this result is installing *WordPress*.

2
Installing WordPress

Stage Tasks

Our goal is to create a working, full-fledged WordPress website.

This website will be completely ready for customization and content filling. This site will have everything you need to get started successfully. There will be nothing superfluous or unnecessary on this site. There will be nothing on this site that will interfere with its operation and your success.

We will install and configure everything that is missing on it later in the following stages.

We could use the hosting service that it offers us and install WordPress directly from cPanel using a special installer and start setting it up right away. Then, install plugins, experiment with themes, and check out different special offers.

It's time to stop before you start doing all this.

Listen to what I tell you.

I have seen a lot of successful projects and participated in many of them. They were successful and brought good income. This has always been the case if the project participants had complete control over everything related to the projects.

I have seen many unsuccessful and outright failed projects. They were a real headache for all participants and brought nothing but grief and loss. This was always the case if the project participants did not fully control them.

The most complete control can be ensured only by the independent execution of all important operations. And installing WordPress is, of course, a very important operation.

WordPress is an open-source system, and any hosting provider can hire programmers to work on customizing WordPress, themes and plugins. This can provide new opportunities and help give your website a unique look and feel.

But this will no longer be an original, authentic product! And this product is highly likely to be connected in some way to the hosting company. And no one knows how it might behave in the future. Moreover, it is unknown what can happen to such a site when changing hosting.

Do you want to run experiments on your site that someone else controls? I don't want to either, and I don't advise you to do that.

Therefore, we choose the most reliable and safe path. We source the WordPress distribution, themes, plugins, and everything else from the official repository on the WordPress developer site.

Now, we will download the WordPress distribution, place it on our server, and unpack it into the site's root directory.

And there is one more important thing that I must remind you of. Don't forget to fill out the Planner!

2.1. Getting WordPress onto the Server

We're getting started with *WordPress*!

2.1.1. Copying WordPress System to the Server

Open the official **WordPress** (**https://wordpress.org**) site. It has a new design that has significantly increased the visibility of the "*Get WordPress*" button. Click this button.

You will be taken to a page with a link to download the current archive with the latest version of the *WordPress* system. Click on this link, and this file will begin downloading to your computer's hard drive in the *Downloads* folder.

Next to this link is another one - to a page describing the installation process. You can open it for review; it will tell you how to do what is described here. There is nothing new or unexpected there; there is a text description for all occasions. Our case is quite simple, so there is no point in reading this universal text.

Open the *Downloads* folder on your computer. In a browser, log into your hosting account, activate *cPanel*, launch *File Manager*, and open the directory with your site files (Figure 2-1). The same directory in which you created the *test.txt* and *.htaccess* files.

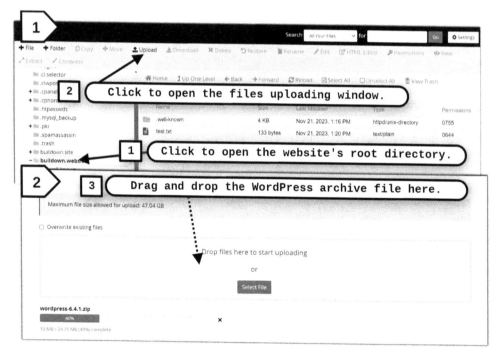

Figure 2-1. Uploading the WordPress archive to the root directory of the website.

On the toolbar, click the *Upload* button. Drag and drop the *WordPress* archive file into the page that opens. Uploading the file to the server will begin immediately. When the process is completed, click on the close page button, and you will automatically return to the directory page with the site files.

2.1.2. Unpacking WordPress System Files on the Server

Now, you need to unpack the archive. To do this, right-click on the file name and select "*Extract*" from the menu that appears. In the window that opens, click the "*Extract Files*" button (Figure 2-2).

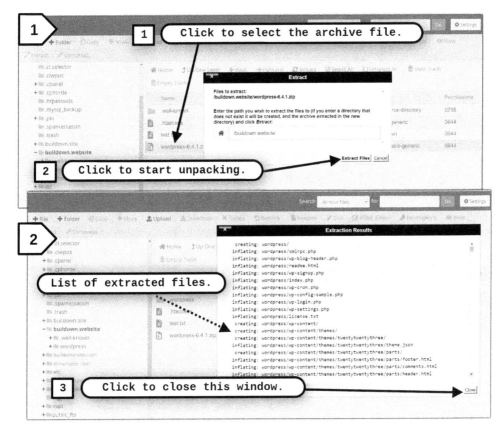

Figure 2-2. Unpacking the WordPress archive in the root directory of the website.

The archive will be unpacked immediately. The extraction results will be shown in the "*Extraction Results*" window. Close this window, and immediately after that, you will find that the archive is unpacked into a separate directory called "W*ordpress*".

There are probably good reasons for developers to create an archive along with this directory, but we don't need it. We need to move all the folders and files nested in this directory to a higher level, that is, to the directory with the files of our site. This will avoid some minor troubles in the future and make it easier to resolve some technical issues.

You will no longer need the "*Wordpress.zip*" archive; after unpacking it, you can simply delete it.

Open the newly created "*Wordpress*" directory and highlight the first line with your mouse; this is the *wp-admin* folder. Press the *Shift* key on your keyboard, and without releasing it, select the last line; this is the *xmlrpc.php* file (Figure 2-3). Release the mouse button and the *Shift* key.

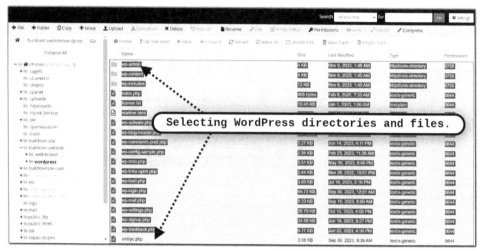

Figure 2-3. Selecting WordPress directories and files.

You've just selected the files and folders that make up the entire *WordPress* system, just like you would select a list of files and folders in *Windows*.

Click on this list, drag it, and drop it into the directory of your site. In the same directory in which you created the *test.txt* file and the *.htaccess* file (Figure 2-4).

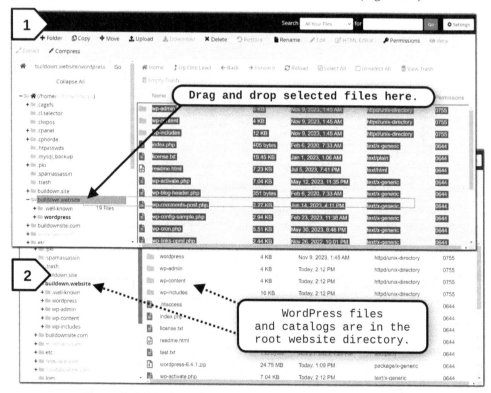

Figure 2-4. Moving selected WordPress directories and files.

Remember? If you have a single domain, then this is the root directory of the site (*public_html*, the one with the globe icon; do not confuse it with the root directory of the host!), and if, like me, this is an added domain, then this is the directory with its name.

After transferring the folders and files of the *WordPress* system, enter the site directory and ensure that the files are indeed where they should be. Then, check the contents of the "*Wordpress*" directory from which you transferred the folders and files. This directory is now empty because all its contents have been moved to the site's root directory.

We no longer need the empty "*Wordpress*" directory and can delete it.

We've just finished a fairly simple job - placing the *WordPress* system in the main directory of the site we're building. At the same time, we continued to study the techniques of working in *File Manager* and found out that we did not encounter anything new or unexpected.

We have very little time left before we start working with the *WordPress* system.

In the next step, we will prepare to install *WordPress*. This is not a very big job, but it must be done correctly and without haste.

2.2. Preparing to Install WordPress

2.2.1. The Last Step Before Installing WordPress

We've reached the last step before installing *WordPress*.

We have completed all the preparatory work. All information about this work was entered into the Planner, right?

Have you read the instructions on the official *WordPress* website for preparing a host and installing *WordPress* on a website? Are you a little confused and don't know exactly what to do?

Close the pages with these instructions. They are written without considering a specific server configuration and, therefore, have a slightly too general character.

We are creating a website on a server with the configuration we need; therefore, we have no doubts about the sequence of actions. We don't have any questions to which we need to look for answers. Consequently, we will proceed very simply.

Keep in mind that all the actions we will now perform are classics. This is the traditional procedure for preparing to launch the installer, as *WordPress* has always had it.

In the latest versions of *WordPress*, these steps may even be ignored, but we will follow them carefully.

2.2.2. Preparing the WordPress Configuration File

The traditional procedure for preparing to install *WordPress* involves manually editing the main configuration file. This file, immediately after unpacking the WordPress archive, has the name *wp-config-sample.php*.

This name can be confusing because this is not actually an example configuration file but an actual, real configuration file. It just doesn't have the database name itself, database username, and password for that database user to access.

That is, the file must contain the same information that we received after creating the database and user account in Chapter 1.8.

This information is traditionally recorded and stored in the *wp-config.php* file. This is the only way to connect the *WordPress* system installed on your site and the site's database.

You, the site owner, need to know exactly how this is done. You must know where the database name, username, and password to access the database should be written. Therefore, we need to open the *wp-config-sample.php* file for editing, paste this information into the right places, save the file with the changes, close the editor, and rename the file (Figure 2-5).

Yes, the *wp-config-sample.php* file will need to be renamed after editing. You need to remove the word "-sample" from its name, and this file will have the name *wp-config.php*, under which the *WordPress* system will use it.

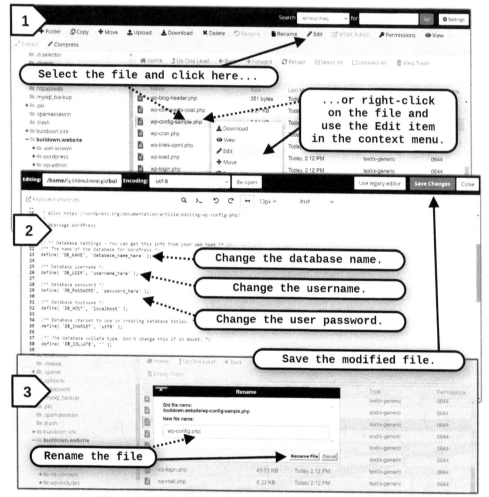

Figure 2-5. Modifying the wp-config-sample.php file.

So, you opened the file and entered the database name, its user name, and the database access password.

Rename the file in a way convenient for you.

As in conventional file management systems, you can do this by selecting the file with one mouse click and then (not too quickly, so as not to double-click) click on its name again. The name line will become editable. Remove anything unnecessary from the file name and press *Enter*.

The second option is also quite common. Call the context menu by right-clicking on the line with the file name. Select "*Rename*" from the menu, correct the file name, and click the "*Rename File*" button.

The main *WordPress* configuration file is now called *wp-config.php*.

A helpful note about double-clicking. The *File Manager* in the *cPanel* console, when you double-click on a directory name, opens it, as we expect. Double-clicking on a file line initiates its downloading to your computer's hard drive rather than calling the editor. So, you just need to get used to it.

Everything is ready to install *WordPress*.

2.3. WordPress Installation

2.3.1. Things to Have on Hand When Installing WordPress

When installing *WordPress*, you will need to have at hand a short name for your site, a nickname (the username of the *WordPress* system of your site; do not confuse this name with the database username; this is a different name!) under which you will log in to *WordPress*, your main address email and password to log into the site management system.

If you have your own password, of course, it's better to come up with it and write it down in advance.

But it must be a strong password!

More than enough people on our planet want to hack *WordPress* sites; there is no need to make their lives easier.

The password can be generated by the installer during the installation process. The installer generates strong passwords, and I recommend that you do not create your own password but save the generated one and use it in the future.

It is best to save the site name, nickname, and email address in advance in some text file or write it down in Planner so as not to make accidental typos or errors (Figure 2-6). During installation, you will simply copy them using the keyboard or rewrite them from a sheet and paste them into the dialog fields.

When choosing a nickname and password, you should never use well-known options like *admin, user, qwerty, 12345*, etc.

These options and their analogs, which were repeatedly invented by people in a hurry and thoughtlessly, have long been in the databases of website hacking programs and are checked by them first.

The best nickname option is your real name and your real last name or other variations of your first and last name, which should not coincide with the name that will be the name of the author, visible to everyone in publications on the site.

They can be separated by a space or connected by an underscore. If you add some symbols or numbers at the end, the security of your nickname will increase significantly. Do this right away because, after installation, it will be impossible to change your nickname.

For example, a good nickname might look like *John_Doe_Not_Now_555* if your name is *John Doe*. A simple nickname will simplify the task of website hackers; a complicated nickname will eliminate this vulnerability.

This nickname will be used to create an administrator account for your site. You will only use it to log in to the site as its administrator.

47

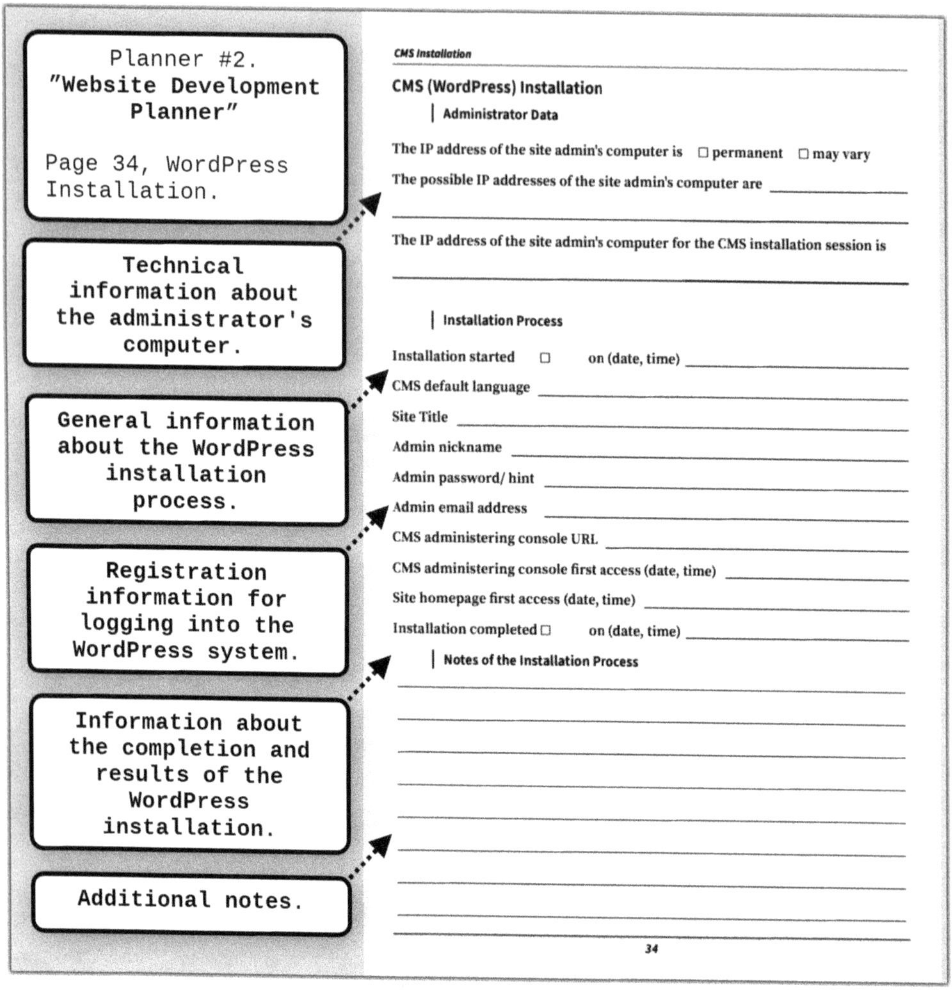

Planner #2.
"Website Development Planner"

Page 34, WordPress Installation.

Technical information about the administrator's computer.

General information about the WordPress installation process.

Registration information for logging into the WordPress system.

Information about the completion and results of the WordPress installation.

Additional notes.

CMS Installation

CMS (WordPress) Installation
| Administrator Data

The IP address of the site admin's computer is ☐ permanent ☐ may vary
The possible IP addresses of the site admin's computer are _____
_____
The IP address of the site admin's computer for the CMS installation session is
_____

| Installation Process

Installation started ☐ on (date, time) _____
CMS default language _____
Site Title _____
Admin nickname _____
Admin password/ hint _____
Admin email address _____
CMS administering console URL _____
CMS administering console first access (date, time) _____
Site homepage first access (date, time) _____
Installation completed ☐ on (date, time) _____

| Notes of the Installation Process

_____
_____
_____
_____
_____
_____
_____
_____
_____

34

Figure 2-6. Getting started with the Website Development Planner.

Later, when setting up *WordPress*, I'll show you what else you need to do with this account. So, are you ready?

2.3.2. Running the WordPress Installer

Then, type the installer's address in the browser's address bar.
For your domain "*your-domain-name.zone*", it is

```
https://your-domain-name.zone/wp-admin/install.php
```

Don't forget to replace "*your-domain-name.zone*" with your real domain name.
As you can see, we are using an address with access via the secure *https* protocol.
When you type the installer address for your site, do not forget to replace the domain name in this line. So, you have entered the installer's address. Press *Enter*.

You will immediately see a window for selecting the language that will be the main language for the site (Figure 2-7). Select the desired language and click the "*Continue*" button.

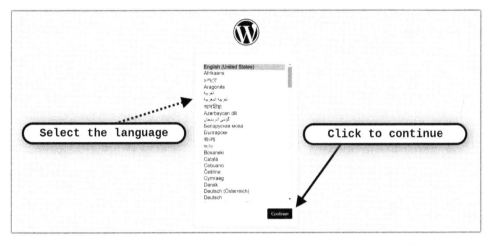

Figure 2-7. WordPress installer window with language selection dialog.

Now, you see the main window with registration information (Figure 2-8).

Fill out all the fields, copy and save (and write down on paper) the password provided by the installer (of course, you can use your own password instead), activate the "*Discourage search engines from indexing this site*" checkbox, and click the "*Install Wordpress*" button.

Installing *WordPress* will only take a couple of seconds.

After this, you will see a successful installation message on the screen and an invitation to start working (Figure 2-9). Click the "*Log In*" link.

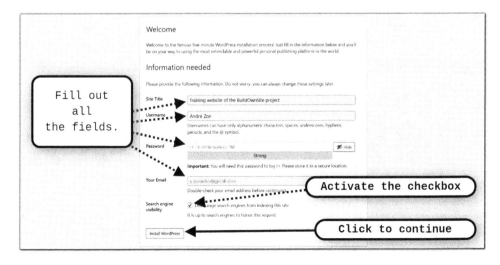

Figure 2-8. WordPress installer window with registration information fields.

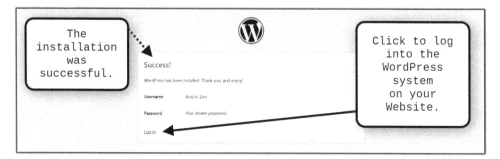

Figure 2-9. WordPress installer window showing job completion notification.

2.3.3. First Login to the WordPress System on the Website

Enter your nickname (*WordPress* username, not your database) and password into the dialog fields (Figure 2-10). Activate the "*Remember Me*" checkbox. This will allow you not to enter your login and password for two weeks when accessing *WordPress* on your site from your computer. Click the "*Log In*" button.

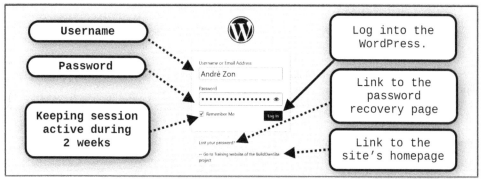

Figure 2-10. WordPress login window.

You'll be immediately taken to *WordPress* on your own site (Figure 2-11).

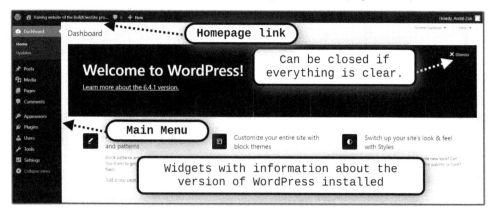

Figure 2-11. WordPress system interface with a link to the website's homepage.

On the top toolbar, on the very left side, next to the *WordPress* icon, you will see the name of your site, and you can click on it to see the main page of your site (Figure 2-12).

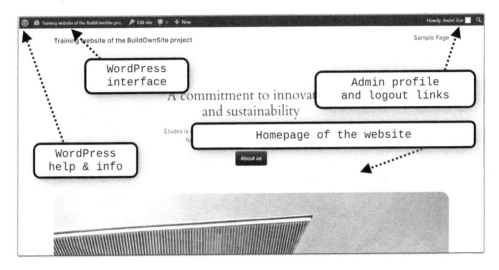

Figure 2-12. Home page of a newly created website.

It is fantastic, right?!

Now, we have to make it a unique masterpiece.

But first, we need to solve priority problems. To know how to do this using *WordPress*, you need to know a little about the system interface and the rules for working with it.

First, save the address of the page you find yourself on in your browser bookmarks. This is the entry point to the *WordPress* system installed on your site. The system will remember you for some time (the standard period is two weeks), after which the active session will expire, and you will need to enter your username and password to log in to your site's management system.

2.4. First Look at the WordPress Interface

2.4.1. Important WordPress Interface Features

The *WordPress* system interface is quite simple, functional, and similar to many interfaces of your usual applications.

But it has its own characteristics. They are critical to know.

In my opinion, the main one of these features is that new elements and even entire blocks of elements can appear in different areas of this interface. They are created by themes and plugins installed on the site. Themes do this relatively rarely, but plugins do this quite often.

Not all theme and plugin authors warn about this. But you should remember and understand now that the *WordPress* interface is not static.

Therefore, you must understand that installing a new plugin or changing a theme should definitely begin with studying the documentation for these plugins and on this theme. Or at least by studying the author's screenshots, usually given along with the description.

For now, we'll take a look at the *WordPress* interface, and I'll tell you where everything is.

2.4.2. WordPress Main Menu and Pages

Immediately after logging into *WordPress*, you will be taken to the *Dashboard* section, the *Home* page (Figure 2-13).

On the *Dashboard/Home* page, after installing *WordPress* and each *WordPress* update, an eye-catching banner appears, indicating the successful completion of the operation.

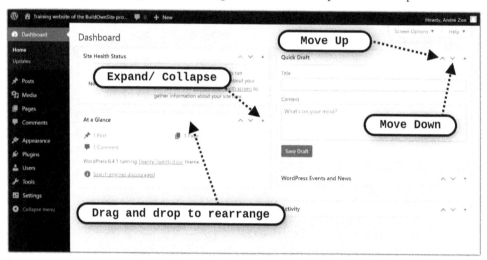

Figure 2-13. The WordPress system interface of a newly created website.

This banner contains a link to a list of new system features. We will not go over it because it is interesting for those who have already worked with the previous version. We'll just close this banner.

In addition to the banner, this page contains blocks with information about the status of the site, recent operations, visitor activity, and events in the *WordPress* community (Figure 2-14). You can collapse these blocks and rearrange them as you wish.

New blocks may appear on this page. They are usually installed by plugins that are important for the site. For example, security plugins. We will see this in the future.

As you might guess, the *Dashboard/Updates* page contains information about available updates and how to manage them. There is nothing here right now because the site has just been created, and all its components are up to date.

As you already understand, the system's main menu is located on the left side of the screen. This sidebar can be collapsed or expanded. This does not affect the operation of the system; it is a matter of your comfort.

At first glance, the main menu looks too simple (Figure 2-15).

There are actually two levels to this menu, and you're only seeing the top one right now. If you simply place your mouse over any menu item, you will see what is on the second level.

The main menu will not always look like it does now. As you install plugins and change the theme, new items can and will appear in it.

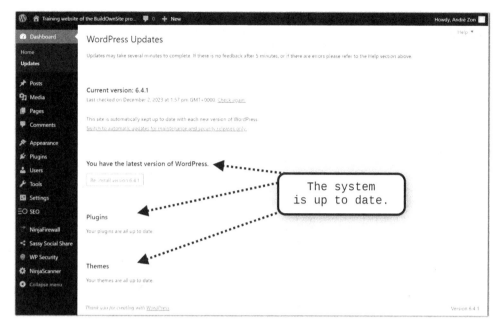

Figure 2-14. The Dashboard/ Updates block interface.

Plugins very often add new items to the main menu, but themes do this quite rarely. New items can be added both to the first level of the menu and to the second. So you need to be careful not to get confused.

Now we will not consider in detail what is hidden behind each menu item. We have a lot more to explore, and we won't miss anything.

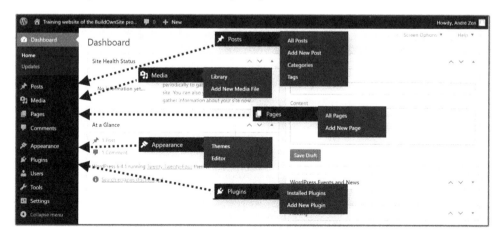

Figure 2-15. Main menu of the system.

The *Post* item deals not only with posts, which make up the bulk of the site's information. Here, you also work with the structural elements of the site - *Categories* and *Tags*.

The *Media* item is, first of all, images. Other types of multimedia resources are used much less frequently in real practice. For example, it is usually more profitable to post videos on external platforms such as *YouTube*. Because it's free. After all, video takes up a lot of disk space and requires a lot of outgoing traffic when playing. On any hosting, it will cost money, even if this hosting is proudly called unlimited.

We move on.

The *Pages* item is separate. This is because *Page* is a type of site page that is not associated with categories, tags, or anything else. This is an entirely self-contained post that simply doesn't need everything that is typically found on a feature post page. The most common uses of pages are for official site information or to create custom page layouts, such as a custom home page layout. It is important. And we will return to the pages more than once.

The *Comments* item, as you might guess, is everything that relates to working with comments. This kind of work is routine and, in my opinion, there is not much interesting in it. Comments are most often simply disabled and blocked by site owners so that they are simply not visible and so that users are not able to comment on publications.

This is due to the massive use of the ability to comment on publications by numerous and diverse spammers.

Links placed in spam comments on your posts can seriously damage the site's reputation. Therefore, you need to understand that leaving the ability to comment is reasonable only if you set up a lot of restrictions and checks, and provided that you can devote enough time to regularly checking and moderating comments.

The *Appearance* item, which now looks very modest, is very important. Here is absolutely everything that determines the appearance of your site. Here you can customize themes, change the appearance of various blocks, create and edit menus, and do much more. The most significant influence on the options available at this point is what theme you have installed on your site. Each theme can add its own items to this menu, and there can be many of them. We will look at this issue in some detail, using a fairly typical theme as an example, in a separate chapter.

Note. Since version 6.1, *WordPress* has actively used block technology. It is now used to create new templates for various types of pages and their parts. This is a very exciting activity, but I do not recommend starting with *WordPress* using this technology. When we look at *WordPress* themes, I'll explain in more detail why I'm making this recommendation.

We continue to get acquainted with the system interface.

The *Plugins* item, of course, is responsible for access to plugin management tools.

The *Users* item is access to the list of users and operations with personnel accounts on your site.

The *Tools* item, as you can see, already contains quite a lot of sub-items compared to other main menu items. The authors of a variety of plugins are very fond of adding additional subparagraphs to this paragraph.

There are also two traditional sub-items in this paragraph - *Theme File Editor* and *Plugin File Editor*. They are intended for those who know how to create and debug programs in *PHP*, and have remained from those distant times when programmers, rather than website owners, dealt with the *WordPress* system much more often.

If you are not a programmer, then you are better off just forgetting about the existence of these menu items. When we configure the plugin responsible for site security, we will return to this issue.

The *Settings* item, as you might guess, is responsible for conservative site settings, which are best done only once. And some of them, such as *Permalinks*, are strictly recommended to be performed only once! We will turn to the sub-items of this menu item very soon.

Many plugins also often add their own lines to the *Settings* item.

We briefly looked at the main menu items.

2.4.3. WordPress Interface Blocks and Work Areas

Now, also briefly, I will tell you about the rest of the *WordPress* interface.

When viewed from left to right, the topmost toolbar contains a *WordPress* drop-down menu, a link to your site's home page, recent comments, and a drop-down menu for adding new posts, media, pages, and users (Figure 2-16). On the right side of the toolbar, there is a drop-down menu with links to the active user profile and a link to log out.

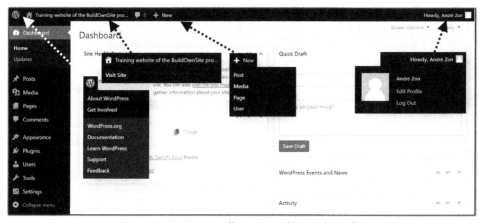

Figure 2-16. Top toolbar, WordPress interface.

This toolbar has two exciting features.

Firstly, some plugins can add their own icons and drop-down menus to it. This is usually quite convenient. Secondly, if you are logged in to the site as an administrator, the toolbar will be displayed just for you not only in the *WordPress* interface but also on regular site pages (Figure 2-17). Remember this feature; you will need to remember it in the future when we evaluate the performance and quality of the site.

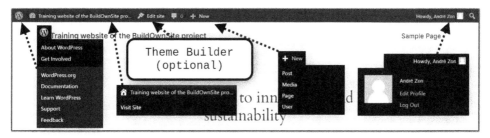

Figure 2-17. Top toolbar, website homepage.

This is not the only component that can be displayed to an authorized administrator on regular site pages. Some plugins display their own elements for ease of use. We will see this again in the future.

All other *WordPress* interface elements are not displayed on regular website pages.Below the top toolbar, there is another toolbar. On it, we see two buttons.Why the *Help* button is needed is clear to everyone. It opens a top panel that contains contextual tooltips and links to documentation and support pages. *Screen Options* button opens the top panel, the contents of which change when working with different system components (Figure 2-18). Plugins can add additional options to this panel.

Please note that this panel allows you to customize the composition of the displayed information not only when working with lists but also when working with their individual elements. This is a very flexible and powerful tool whose existence is worth remembering.

Figure 2-18. Top panel with screen options.

As you already understand, the most interesting things happen in the main area of the browser window, located in the center of the screen (Figure 2-19).

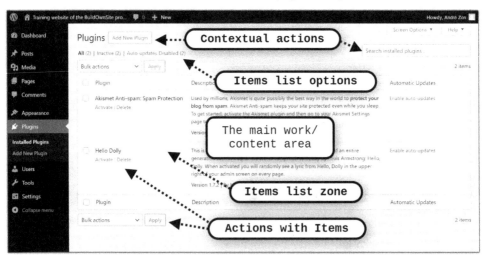

Figure 2-19. The main work/ content area.

Lists of plugins and publications are displayed here, and settings, various fields, texts, and buttons are contained. Everything that corresponds to the main menu item you selected is located in the left sidebar.

There is one more working area of the screen that you need to learn how to work with. This is the right sidebar (Figure 2-20). It appears when you add or edit posts and pages. This is where you'll find all the features and settings that apply to the post or page you're working with.

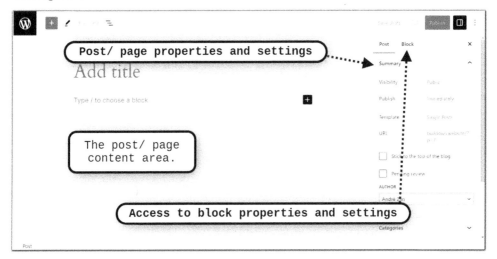

Figure 2-20. The right sidebar area.

What you're currently seeing is this part of the interface for the version of the Block Editor that *WordPress* currently comes with by default. After installing the standard editor, you will see that all this may look different.

So, we have made a general overview of the interface. Now you know what it consists of. A detailed acquaintance with different parts of the interface awaits us in the process of practical work.

Now that we understand the system, we must perform some necessary steps.

We will configure the most important features of your website.

2.5. Initial WordPress Settings

2.5.1. Where are the Settings Located?

We have already completed the very first parameter setup of our website.

If you remember, when installing *WordPress*, we activated the "*Discourage search engines from indexing this site*" checkbox in the installer dialog.

This means that in the internal data of all site pages, which is usually called "metadata", the word "noindex" is written in a special field. It alerts search engines that the site is not yet ready for indexing.

If we did not do this, pages on our site that contain temporary information could be indexed by the *Google* search engine. All our subsequent actions to change the content of pages and remove test pages that accidentally appeared in the search could lead to some decrease in the site's reputation.

Search engines should see only high-quality content. Therefore, the best solution at the site creation stage is to close the site from indexing.

Let's check how we did it. Open the *Settings/Reading* page. As you can see, at the bottom of the *"Search engine visibility"* block, the *"Discourage search engines from indexing this site"* checkbox is already activated (Figure 2-21). This is the same setting that we enabled during the *WordPress* installation process.

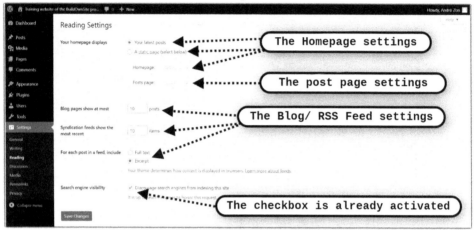

Figure 2-21. Settings/ Reading page

Since we've landed on this page, let's perform the necessary actions on it. We go from top to bottom.

2.5.2. Home Page and Other Reading Settings

The *"Your homepage displays"* block allows you to choose one of two options.

The *"Your latest posts"* option is the most popular. If you choose it, your latest posts will always be at the top of the site's home page. No additional effort is required on your part. This widespread choice has one very serious drawback, which not all owners of their own websites seriously think about.

The fact is that many themes with such a home page layout setup do not have a main post. This means that there is maybe no tag on the home page, known as the *H1* tag (or *h1*, they are the same thing). Remember this now, even if you have no idea what we are talking about.

The most important thing to know about this tag is that it contains a title that applies to the entire page. In this case - to the entire home page. To the very page from which search engines begin indexing the entire site.

How do you think search engines will feel about a site's home page if they can't figure out what it's called because it doesn't have a title?

You probably understood everything correctly. They will treat it badly. And this will entail not very good consequences for the entire site.

We will return to this issue when we choose a theme and configure the site structure. For now, just remember this.

The *"Blog pages show at most"* setting specifies the number of posts that should be displayed on the home page, category pages, search results, and other feeds. In the future, you can simply overcome this number experimentally.

Recommendation for the future: there should be a maximum number of posts that does not critically reduce page loading speed. Leave this setting as it is for now.

The "*Syndication feeds show the most recent*" setting specifies the number of posts that will be contained in the *RSS* feeds. This is a special form of a site's publications that can be used by owners of other sites to import your publications. If you don't know what this is about yet, then just don't change this setting.

If you don't want anyone to be able to import your content in its entirety, which is quite reasonable, then set the "*For each post in a feed, include*" switch to the "*Excerpt*" position. Now, if someone imports your content, they will receive the title of the post, its short description, and a link to the full version of the post. It can even be good for your website.

Click the "*Save Changes*" button. Now, you need to check and correct a few more settings related to the site as a whole and its main page.

Open the *Settings/General* page. You don't need to change anything here; just enter a short site description in the *Tagline* line. And, if necessary, change regional settings. Click the "*Save Changes*" button. Now you know where the *WordPress* settings menu is and how to work with it. Let's continue with other settings.

2.5.3. Settings That Affect Each Post

Go ahead. Open the *Settings/Writing* page (Figure 2-22).

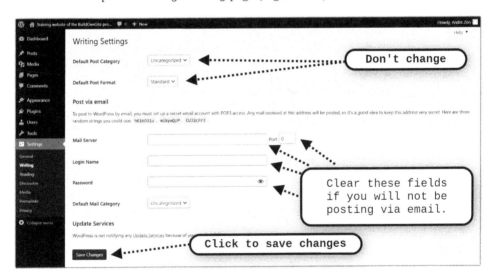

Figure 2-22. Settings/ Writing page.

There is simply nothing to change here now. There are no categories on the site yet, and we don't know whether the *Default* post format needs to be changed.

Do you think you might someday need to be able to publish posts via email? This feature has traditionally existed in this system since the days when the sound produced by the modem could control the Internet connection. In any case, you definitely don't need it now. If such a need arises, you now know where to find the settings to use it.

Open the *Settings/Discussion* page (Figure 2-23). Some pretty obvious things are written here that you can configure if you need user comments on your site.

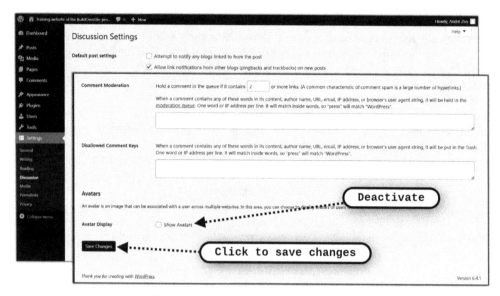

Figure 2-23. Settings/ Discussion page.

Now, you just need to keep two things in mind. Firstly. If you leave the "*Show Avatars*" checkbox activated, their use will slow down the website pages.

Secondly. If you decide to disable the ability to comment on posts, the easiest way to do this is using a special plugin, which is very popular for good reason. I warned you about spammers, do you remember? At the initial stage of your project, when you are creating a website and just starting to fill it with content, it is probably better to disable comments. And then, in the future, you will make your own decision.

Open the *Settings/Media* page (Figure 2-24). Look through it and just remember this page.

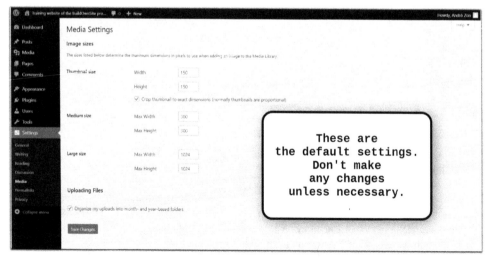

Figure 2-24. Settings/ Media page.

The need to change something here rarely arises. This happens if you are using some very special theme. As for the automatic storage of illustrations in folders by year and month of publication, this is very convenient. In general, here, you can leave everything as is.

And on the *Settings/ Permalinks* page (Figure 2-25), it is advisable to change the settings and change them quite radically. This issue must be taken very seriously. It's best never to change the settings you make here after the site is indexed by search engines. If you change them after indexing, the site will inevitably lose its position in the search.

That's what we're talking about.

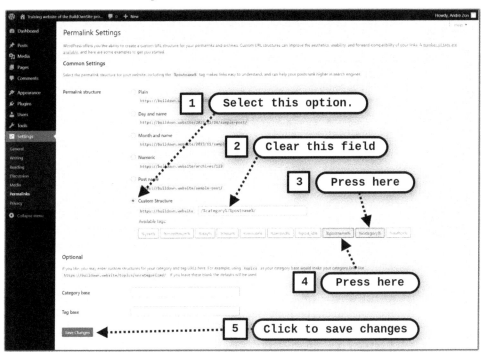

Figure 2-25. Settings/ Permalinks page.

By default, the system generates the address of your publications from the year, month, and day and, at the very end, adds a line formed from the post's title.

This is not a very good option. It would be much better if there was a category name instead of numbers and slashes in front of the post title. Surely category names on a themed site are keywords, right?

In general, I recommend that you do what you now see on the screen.

Click the *Custom Structure* radio button. In the "*Available tags*" button row, deactivate all buttons. The address format will be cleared. Click the "*Category*" button and then the "*Postname*" button.

You have now created the post address format that search engines like best.

Never change it.

Click the "*Save Changes*" button.

There is one more point left. Open the *Settings/Privacy* page (Figure 2-26).

This point does not concern you personally or the configuration of your site.

This point is needed to create an official and somewhat formal page, which should be on every website.

In the *Settings* tab, you can create new pages that will be used in this role on your site and switch them as needed. This is very convenient when making changes to a site's privacy policy.

Just remember to disable indexing of such pages when they are ready to be published.

On the *Policy Guide* tab, you will see general rules for filling out pages with privacy policies, and you can get a ready-made template.

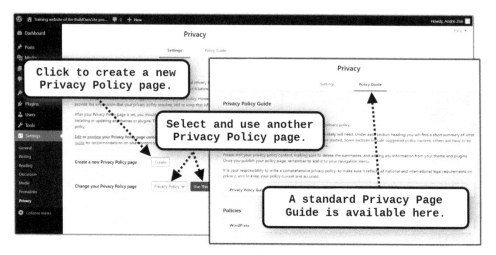

Figure 2-26. Settings/ Privacy Policy page.

We will definitely remember this when we create the official pages of the site.

Now, we have finished working with the site's basic settings and will check its health.

2.6. Checking the Website Health

2.6.1. What Is Website Health, and What Needs to Be Done Now

The general technical condition of the site, which for brevity is called its health, consists of a large number of parameters and indicators.

You can check it in various ways. There are many tools and services for this that you will undoubtedly come across someday.

Now, we will use the simplest, most accessible, and most understandable verification methods to ensure everything is going according to plan and everything is fine with our site.

Let's open the *Tools/ Site Health* page (Figure 2-27).

The site status check will begin immediately without additional steps. The verification time is usually a few seconds, but sometimes you need to wait a little longer.

Our site has just been created. It has a very simple configuration, and therefore, the verification is completed very quickly.

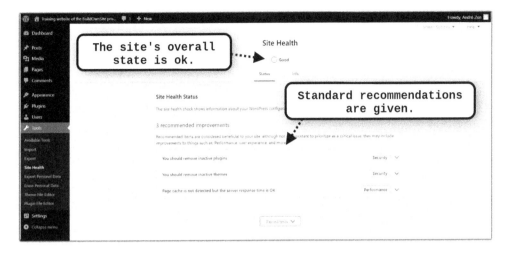

Figure 2-27. Tools/ Site Health page.

That's what we see here. On the *Status* tab, the system reports that everything is fine with our site, and the green indicator in the form of a circle is almost closed. So, are there still any problems?

Nothing threatening or severe. The system recommends that we remove unused themes and inactive plugins. This is a universal recommendation. The fewer themes and plugins installed on a site, the better for its security.

We will now implement these recommendations.

2.6.2. Removing Unused and Inactive Plugins

Let's open the *Plugins/ Installed Plugins* page (Figure 2-28). There are actually two plugins here, and both are greyed out.

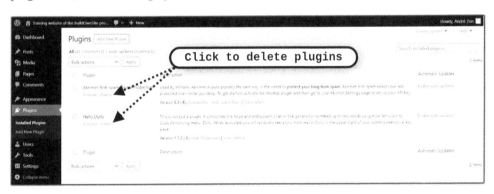

Figure 2-28. Plugins/ Installed Plugins page.

The *Hello Dolly* plugin has a short description that says it all. It's just a little toy that developers traditionally include in the *WordPress* distribution. We'll remove this plugin now because we definitely won't need it. If you want, you can admire its work on your website.

On the contrary, the *Akismet Anti-Spam* plugin is very helpful. But it is only needed if comments are activated on the site. You and I will not use them, so this plugin will also be removed. If you decide to allow comments on your site, then this plugin may come in handy. We are now more interested in the purity of the experiment; we want to find out the effect of inactive plugins on the site's health indicators. Therefore, we will remove this plugin as well.

Plugins can be removed individually or in a list. I always carry out critical operations separately to avoid making any mistakes due to haste or inattention. I recommend that you follow this rule, too.

So, we remove the plugins one by one. Ready. There are no inactive plugins on our site.

2.6.3. Removing Inactive Themes

Now, let's open the *Appearance/ Themes* page (Figure 2-29). There are three themes here. These themes are created by a *WordPress* developer and are always included in the distribution. More precisely, it includes three themes that were most recently developed. The newest one is automatically activated when the site is created.

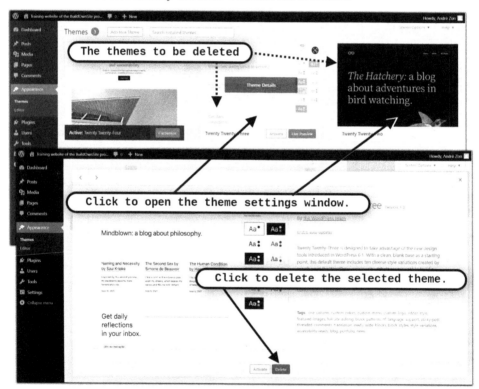

Figure 2-29. Appearance/Themes page.

The *WordPress* developer traditionally names standard themes based on the year they were developed. If you want, you can find themes from previous years on the official *WordPress* website, and maybe one of them will be suitable for your site.

When writing this book edition, the first official partially-block theme, "Twenty Twenty-Three," was active, and since WordPress Version 6.4.1, the Twenty Twenty-Four" was added. This is the first official full-featured block-style theme, and we will touch on block design more in the future. Therefore, we will leave this theme active; it may be helpful for us to study the features of block technology.

We will delete all other themes.

Advice for the future. When you choose, install, activate, and customize a theme for your site, it will most likely be a third-party theme rather than a *WordPress* developer theme.

Although the site health checker will tell you to keep just one theme and delete the rest, don't do it.

The fact is that incomplete compatibility of *WordPress* themes and plugins can cause problems and even lead to website inoperability. This rarely happens, but it is better to foresee this situation in advance.

Therefore, if suddenly, after installing or updating a plugin on the site, problems begin, you can immediately switch to using a backup theme to make sure that the guess about the plugin incompatibility is correct. After this, you will decide to deactivate the problematic plugin or change the theme. Typically, such situations lead to removing and replacing the plugin with another similar plugin.

As a backup theme, it is best to leave some official theme from the *WordPress* developer. Ideally, this is the theme you should start customizing the appearance and functionality of your site with. This understanding and skill will come to you with experience.

And we will continue our experiment with improving the health of the site. We removed all plugins and left only one theme on the site.

2.6.4. Rechecking Website Health and Further Actions

Let's open the *Tools/ Site Health* page (Figure 2-30).

As we see, the picture has changed. The system believes that the health of our site has improved.

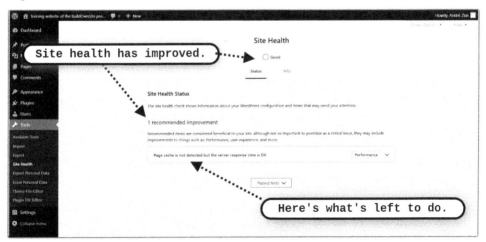

Figure 2-30. Tools/ Site Health page after deleting themes and plugins.

But there was one message left: "*Page cache is not detected, but the server response time is OK.*"

Something went wrong, do you think?

You are mistaken. It's okay. It is better to begin to understand this message from the end.

Here's what we learn from it. The server response time is quite good because the server is fast. But some page cache was not found. What does it mean?

In our case, this means that we simply have not yet installed and configured a special caching plugin. The use of such plugins is a generally accepted and even mandatory practice. And here is the reason.

Every time a visitor opens a page on your site, WordPress assembles that page piece by piece. It takes its fragments from different folders, requests texts and codes from the database, puts everything together, applies styles to the resulting page, and performs various checks and settings, which we won't even discuss now. And, of course, inserts illustrations and various decorative elements.

Do you understand the principle?

This method of creating website pages is called dynamic. This is a very good and convenient method, and this is the method used by the *WordPress* system.

However, this method requires a large amount of server resources, and page generation can take many seconds. This is all very bad. If a lot of visitors come to such a site, then you will go broke paying for hosting. If visitors wait too long for the page they want to load, they will go to your competitor.

If the site health checker knows about it, then search engines will know about it, too. And your site will never get into the top list of search results, which has long been occupied by high-speed pages of other sites.

You are probably already scared enough to feel significant relief after the next phrase. This is the phrase.

All these troubles can be avoided quickly, easily, and free of charge. And we will do it.

We will, of course, install the caching plugin and configure it at the right time.

2.6.5. Complete technical information about the website

Now, we will continue working with the *Tools/ Site Health* page. Actually, it's not even a job. You just need to know about the existence of the *Info* tab and how it is helpful (Figure 2-31).

Let's click on this tab. Here, you can find complete technical information about the site. There are no passwords or other confidential data.

This information can and should be copied to a clipboard and saved as a separate text file. This file can be a very valuable source of information if you need to inspect site configuration changes for diagnostic purposes or in emergency situations.

But it won't come to that if you carefully study this book and follow the recommendations.

But save the file anyway. And don't forget to make a note about it in the Planner.

2.6.6. First Test Using Core Web Vitals

Now, let's do one more check. To do this, we first turn to a tool from *Google* that measures *Core Web Vitals*.

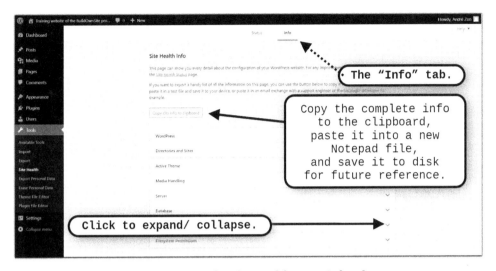

Figure 2-31. Tools/ Site Health page, Info tab.

This tool is called Lighthouse, and it is very convenient to have as an extension in the *Google Chrome* browser (Figure 2-32). This is perhaps the most authoritative source of information about the site's quality, as the outside world sees it, and most importantly, search engines. Find it at

`https://chrome.google.com/webstore/category/extensions`,

install, and activate.

Open the site's main page and click on the *Lighthouse* plugin icon. A small window will open where you must click the "*Generate report*" button.

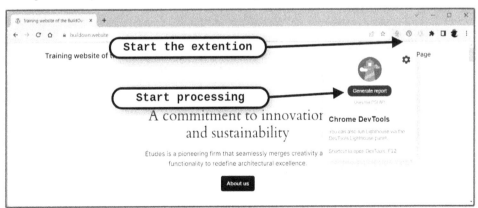

Figure 2-32. Measuring Core Web Vital scores using the Lighthouse.

You will see what *Google* thinks about your site in a few seconds (Figure 2-33). We see excellent results for the first three indicators: 100 points out of 100 possible! This is very good and means we have a very, very fast site!

Figure 2-33. Core Web Vitals scores measured with Lighthouse.

True, this is caused not only by the correctness of our actions but also by the fact that our site is completely empty. There is nothing published on it, and there are almost no components.

When all this appears, the site will begin to work slower, and this will cause a decrease in performance. But this problem can also be solved, and by the time the site is launched, I will teach you how to do that.

But what about the last indicator, such an important indicator, which is designated by the well-known word *SEO*? Why is it so low?

Everything is very simple.

We have not yet installed plugins to solve *SEO* problems, and the demo post automatically generated by the system does not have a *"description"* meta tag. After installing the plugin, we will solve this issue and learn everything about working with meta tags while creating site content.

The message *"Links are not crawlable"* also refers to the content of the demo post, or more precisely, to the green button, which is an active hyperlink but does not contain any address. Hyperlinks should not be like this; we will never create test buttons like this.

And finally, the last point tells us that the site page is closed from indexing. Of course, it's closed. We have closed the site from premature indexing and will open it only when it is ready to index.

And before opening the site, the *SEO* point of the site will also be equal to 100.

Everything is clear with the point system. The site works great and will work even better.

What does the gray circle with the inscription *PWA* mean? Oh, this is a very good thing, and it will also be on our site.

This is a *"Progressive Web Application"* - a technology that allows the site to become a full member of the collection of applications on any smartphone without additional effort on our part. This feature will also come up when we configure the site.

So, we have no unclear or unresolved questions left.

Let's do one more check to make sure everything is done correctly.

When we set up hosting, and checked *DNS* records, and the *SSL* connection, we were tasked with ensuring that the site would work without the *www* prefix and only using the secure *https* protocol.

We needed to ensure that the site pages always opened the same way, regardless of which version of the address the visitor was trying to open.

To check this, we will open the site's main page using a link in the *WordPress* toolbar.

A page opened with an address without *www* and using the *https* protocol. Add *www* to the address and press Enter. We ended up on the same page. Now let's try options with *www* and without *www* using the insecure *http* protocol.

As you can see, the browser, in all cases, redirects us to the page using the secure *https* protocol and without the *www* prefix.

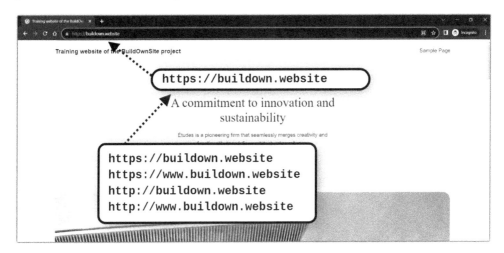

Figure 2-34. Accessing the website with and without the www prefix and both protocols.

This means that we have solved this problem correctly. The site always uses a secure protocol and the same domain. There will be no complaints or quibbles about duplicate pages or using an insecure protocol for the site.

So, it's time to sum up the work of the second stage of website development.

Stage Results

We started the second stage of work on an empty host. We had a specific goal: to create a well-functioning *WordPress* site that does not yet contain any content or additional components.

We downloaded the *WordPress* distributive, uploaded it to the host, unpacked the archive, and moved the system folders and files to the desired location.

We checked that *WordPress* was ready to install and made the necessary changes to the system files.

We installed *WordPress*, logged into the site management system with a real username and password, and ensured the management system and the site's main page opened successfully.

We got acquainted with all parts of the *WordPress* interface, found out their purpose, and found out the features of their use.

We have made the very first and most important settings of the system and website, including those that will never change again.

We checked and even slightly improved the health of the site and stored complete information about its configuration in a separate file.

We checked the speed and quality of the site using the primary tool from *Google* and also learned about what *PWA* is.

We have ensured the site operates using a secure protocol, and its pages cannot be duplicated under different addresses.

Finally, we have conscientiously recorded all the information about the work performed in the Planner, right?

The next stage of work on the site is its configuration. In this case, we mean one of the most favorite activities of all novice *WordPress* website owners - installing and configuring plugins.

3

Configuring
the WordPress Website

Stage tasks

We are starting the third stage of work on creating your website.

You already have the site itself, but it is like a baby. It is small, defenseless, it can't do anything, it doesn't know its capabilities, and it has no one but you.

Don't you really want to help it become big and powerful as soon as possible?

This is just what we will do now.

We will protect the site and teach it to do everything it should be able to do.

The leading role at this stage is given to plugins. There are publications about them on the project's information website; Be sure to read them if you haven't already

We continue our work, believing you already have a general idea of what a plugin is.

If you are an attentive reader, then you already know that I will not do reviews and comparisons, and I will not give advice on choosing and searching for plugins; I will not express my opinion and talk about the advantages and disadvantages of plugins.

I installed and reviewed many plugins, tested them, and monitored their compatibility with each other. It was quite a lot of work, and I will not shift it to you, forcing you to waste time solving problems that I have already solved. I will simply share my experience, and you will start using the plugins that I will tell you about.

In the future, based on this experience, you will be able to work with any plugins more confidently than based on any reviews, comparisons, and advice.

You will soon learn and understand what to do if you decide to use other plugins instead of the ones we will study here and how to add additional plugins to your site.

So, these are the problems we have to solve.

The most important and priority task is to ensure the site's security. It cannot be fully resolved using plugins alone. So, first, we will learn what needs to be done before installing plugins.

Then, we will install and configure plugins that will reliably protect the site from many possible troubles and block attempts by intruders and malware to hack the site, introduce dangerous codes into it, and do many unnecessary things in the same spirit.

After that, we will close the site to visitors so that it does not attract the attention of people and search engines until it is ready for this.

Once the site is fully protected, we will install and configure plugins that will increase site performance and improve indicators that are important to search engines.

Then, we will install and configure plugins that are responsible for solving SEO problems. We will learn the basic rules for using these plugins.

After this, we will install several auxiliary but very important plugins to make your work on the site content easier and more efficient.

Finally, we will add plugins that expand the site's functionality and make it more user-friendly for visitors.

So here we go.

As you install and configure plugins, don't forget to keep the Planner handy and document your actions.

Keep in mind that we will now be installing plugins that are a priority. In the future, we will add some more plugins that will be needed to solve more advanced problems.

3.1. Editing the Administrator Account

Open the *Users/All Users* page (Figure 3-1). This page displays a list of registered users of the site, and there is currently only one line in this list. In this line, one and only account is yours, and you are designated as an administrator in it.

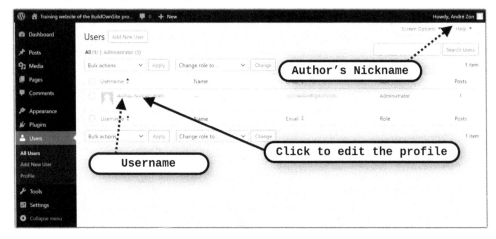

Figure 3-1. Users/ All Users.

We did not open this page to add new users. We need to change your account a little.

The fact is that by default the login matches the name of the author of the publications. When installing *WordPress*, the author name is created automatically, and at this stage, you have no control over this issue.

The dialog you see on the screen when you install *WordPress* doesn't even include a field with the author's name. Maybe the developers simply forgot about this, but a more reasonable explanation is that the site administrator does not have to be the author.

One way or another, the login and author's name are the same. Open an administrator account and you will see this (Figure 3-2).

It would seem - is there any problem here? It turns out there is a problem.

The fact is that people who hack websites are well aware of this coincidence. All they have to do is find out the author's name, which is usually visible or easily accessible even if

72

it is not displayed on the site, and they will know the login to log into the *WordPress* interface on your site. To hack, all they have to do is only guess or intercept the password.

Let's not make it easy for them. You need to make sure that the login and the name of the author of the publications do not match. Fortunately, this is very easy to do.

"*Username cannot be changed.*" This means that we cannot change the login, but this is not necessary. At the stage of creating the site, we deliberately complicated it, remember?

We need to specify a value in the *Nickname* line that does not match the login, then select it in the "*Display name publicly as*" list, and click the "*Update Profile*" button.

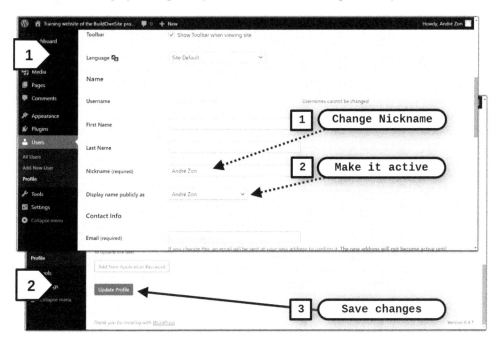

Figure 3-2. Users/ All Users/ Profile.

Ready. We have closed this hole in the site's security.

There is one more action that needs to be performed. It is necessary to close other equally huge holes in the site's security. We will do this using the *.htaccess* file you already know.

3.2. Modifying the .htaccess File

How can the *.htaccess* file be useful for website security?

He has a lot of opportunities for this. We will gradually become acquainted with them when the need arises.

Now, we will need to insert two pieces of code into this file that restrict access to site files.

Open the *.htaccess* file for editing. As you can see, *WordPress* has added its own code snippet to it. We will never do anything with this piece of code.

We need to solve two problems.

Firstly, the *wp_config.php* file contains the name of the site's database, as well as the username and password to access it. If an attacker manages to bypass standard hosting and *WordPress* system security measures, he can gain access to the site's database. This will mean full access to the site. You probably understand what this means. You could lose everything.

Therefore, we will completely block access to this file from anywhere outside. This is done using the first piece of code. You will not need to edit this fragment in the future.

```
# Denied third-party access to wp-config.php file
<files wp-config.php>
order Allow, Deny
Deny from all
</files>
```

This will not affect access to the *wp-config.php* file from your site itself and the *WordPress* system installed on it. And, of course, you can always remove or modify this code if necessary because you have full access to the *.htaccess* file using the *CPanel/ File Manager* application.

Secondly, the most common way to hack websites is to guess the login password in the usual way. To do this, the attacker needs to know the login, which we separated from the author's name in the previous step. However, if the login has already been compromised, hacking also requires an entry point and the ability to guess a password.

The entry point is the full address you enter when logging in to the site. When authorizing, the *wp_login.php* file is used. This file is often renamed in a unique way; captcha and hidden fields are added to it. We don't currently have the right plugin installed for this so we can do it much simpler and, frankly, more efficiently.

We will block access to the login file from all *IP* addresses except ours. If it is unknown to you, you can always find it out using, for example, the request "*my IP address*" entered into the address bar of the *Google Chrome* browser. If you use a *VPN*, you will need the server's address you are connected to.

In the code block, replace the test address *255.255.255.255* with your actual *IP* address.

```
# Limited access to wp-login.php file
<files wp-login.php>
order Deny,Allow
Deny from all
Allow from 255.255.255.255
</files>
```

If you are running your site from multiple addresses or are not working alone, you may need to allow access to *WordPress* from all *IP* addresses used.

In this block of code, you can add the required number of identical lines of the *Allow* operator with all your *IP* addresses.

```
# Limited access to wp-login.php file
<files wp-login.php>
order Deny,Allow
Deny from all
Allow from 255.255.255.255
Allow from 222.222.222.222
Allow from 111.111.111.111
</files>
```

If you have a few IP addresses in use, you can write them in one line of the Allow statement, separating them from each other with one space.

```
# Limited access to wp-login.php file
<files wp-login.php>
order Deny,Allow
Deny from all
Allow from 255.255.255.255 222.222.222.222 111.111.111.111
</files>
```

If you do not want or are not ready for this method of restriction, then pay attention to the "#" symbol at the beginning of the very first line of the above code block.

This character turns a line of code in a .*htaccess* file into a comment line, in which case, if the line contains an actual command, it simply will not be executed. If you want to save some code in the .*htaccess* file for later but do not intend to use it yet, put a "#" character at the beginning of each line of such code.

To make the command lines in the .*htaccess* file active again, you just need to remove such characters and, of course, save the changed file.

Please note that "#" characters in lines that are truly regular comments and not commands, cannot be removed. The system simply will not understand arbitrary text instead of real commands. The .*htaccess* file is very sensitive to any errors!

If its handler encounters a line in which the command is written incorrectly or there is simply text that is not a command, then your site will simply stop working and you will have to return this file to its original state.

Therefore, you need to be very careful when editing the .*htaccess* file. In the future, when your .*htaccess* file becomes long, it will be difficult for you to visually check that the codes are being written correctly.

Therefore, before each editing of this file, it is recommended to download a backup copy of it or make a duplicate of its previous version under a different name directly in the root directory of the site.

So, paste the code, enter your *IP* address in it, make sure that all the comment characters at the beginning of the lines are in the right place, and save the file. Open the home page of your site and the *WordPress* interface in different browser tabs.

All pages open and everything works correctly. This means that the changes in the .*htaccess* file do not contain errors.

We can continue configuring the site.

3.3. Installing and Configuring Security Plugins

3.3.1. Installing the Multipurpose Plugin for Website Protection

Now that we have completed the most straightforward and obvious steps, we can calmly and without haste install the necessary plugins.

We'll start with a universal plugin that can solve a huge number of security problems. In our case, this is the "*All In One WP Security*" ("*AIO WP Security*" for short) plugin.

It is free, has a clear interface, can be configured once, solves all known problems, works reliably, and does not slow down the site. For a fee, you can, if necessary, buy its extensions to solve complex problems professionally. The free version is enough for us for now.

Open the *Plugins/ Add New* page (Figure 3-3). Start typing the name of the plugin in the search bar, and it will appear in the search results pretty quickly. Click the "*Install Now*" button.

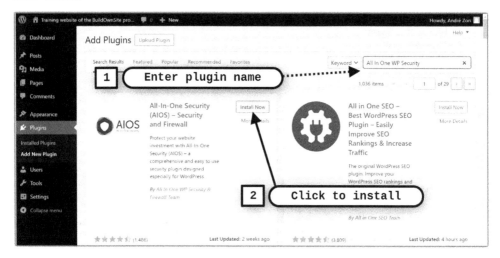

Figure 3-3. WordPress Plugins/Add New: search and install the plugin.

The installation will begin immediately, last a few seconds, and end with the button changing to "*Activate*." Click this button, and the plugin will start working, and the label on the button will change to "*Active*."

The button itself will become inactive (Figure 3-4).

Figure 3-4. WordPress Plugins/Add New: plugin activation.

By the way, this is how plugins are installed from the official *WordPress* repository. Very simple, isn't it?

Open the *Plugins/ Installed Plugins* page (Figure 3-5). Our site's plugins table has just one row, and it shows the plugin we just installed. Click on the "*Settings*" link, and the plugin settings management interface will open in the browser window.

Please note: this plugin adds a link to its own menu to the left sidebar of the system. We will work with all menu items.

The plugin interface has very detailed comments, and I will provide the necessary explanations when it is really necessary.

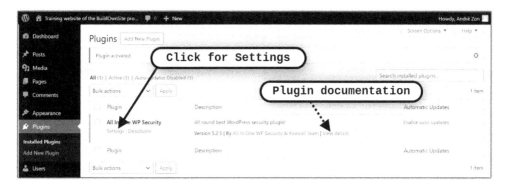

Figure 3-5. Plugins/Installed Plugins/AIO WP Security, links to use.

3.3.2. Setting Up the AIO WP Security Plugin

There is no need to change anything in the "*WP Security/Settings*" item; it is already configured correctly out of the box for typical cases, such as our site. Just look at the tabs and remember their purpose.

Let's move on to the "*WP Security/ Dashboard*" item (Figure 3-6). As expected, there is general information about the site's security status and even a beautiful arrow indicator.

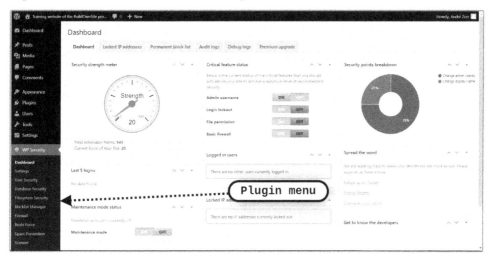

Figure 3-6. WP Security/ Dashboard.

Advice for the future: do not try to achieve the maximum values of this indicator, especially at the initial stage of the site's existence. In the future, when you already feel confident enough to turn your site into a starship, you will definitely return to this issue.

For now, keep in mind that even with settings that will be rated at 200-250 points, this plugin will protect your site quite seriously. We'll even have to disable it for a few minutes when we go to set up the *SEO* plugin.

Warning. Do not use the "*Maintenance mode*" feature of this plugin. This feature may make the site unusable in some cases. We will install another plugin a little later to hide the site from visitors and activate the "*Under construction*" mode.

On the "*WP Security/User Security*" page (Figure 3-7), you will find pretty nice messages telling you that your admin username and author username are secure. This is the result of the right actions we have already taken before.

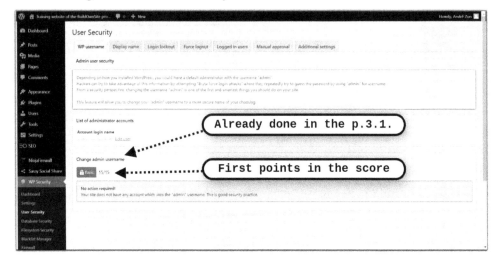

Figure 3-7. WP Security/ User Security.

On the "*WP Security/Display Name*" page, everything is quite clear and configured correctly when installing the plugin. For now, just look at the tabs you'll see there so you know what settings are located here.

Now, repeat the plugin settings described below, and that will be enough for now.

Please note that each setting may add a different number to your total points. These numbers form the indicator that you can see on the "*WP Security/ Dashboard*" page.

On the "*WP Security/ User Security/ Manual approval*" page (Figure 3-8), we activate a checkbox that includes the option to manually confirm a new user registration.

Figure 3-8. WP Security/ User Security/ Manual Approval.

Now, even the most advanced attackers cannot register on the site without the permission of the administrator, that is, you. In this case, the remaining settings on this page are simply not needed.

You can do nothing on the "*WP Security/ Database Security*" page.

The recommended tools for working with database backups will also not be needed because we will do this directly and manually. It's very simple and guarantees complete safety. When you study the issues of maintaining a site in the corresponding volume of this series, you will see this for yourself.

In general, I want to tell you that unnecessary plugins and additions to them are precisely what you should not get carried away with. Many inexperienced website owners have the idea that to solve every problem, you can find a plugin that will do everything itself.

Don't think like that. Plugins are needed only where you absolutely cannot do without them.

However, let's perform the recommended operation of changing the prefix of database tables.

Before executing it, just in case, it is better to create a backup copy of the database (which, if you do everything correctly, you will not need). If something goes wrong, restoring a working version of the database will be very easy.

For the first time, we will make a backup using standard means - using *cPanel*. It's very simple. Let's open the *phpMyAdmin* application, find the desired database, open the *Export* tab, and click the *Go* button (Figure 3-9).

The database backup immediately begins downloading to the *Downloads* folder on your computer. This always happens. The database is very small because the site is empty now, and downloading is fast.

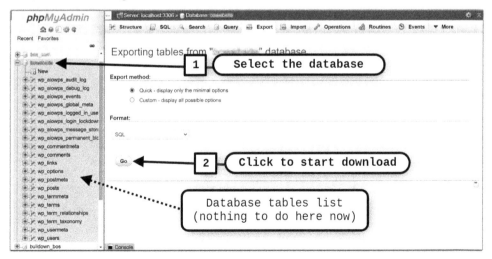

Figure 3-9. cPanel/Database phpMyAdmin page.

To change the prefix (Figure 3-10), you can specify your option or activate the checkbox to generate a sequence of characters automatically.

We selected the automatic option, and the plugin started and finished the renaming operation almost immediately.

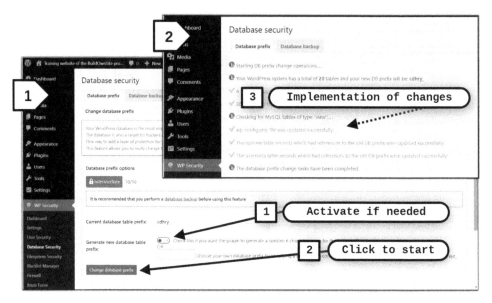

Figure 3-10. WP Security/ Database Security.

Let's open the database in the cPanel again, and look at the prefixes - they have been changed.

Let's go back to the plugin *Dashboard* page and reload it (Figure 3-11). The message about the need to change the prefix has disappeared. The site security score indicator now shows 50.

Figure 3-11. WP Security/ Dashboard: updated security score.

On the "*WP Security/ Filesystem Security*" page (Figure 3-12), you also need to do something.

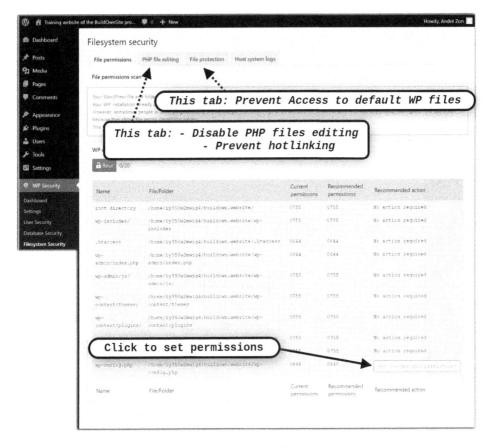

Figure 3-12. WP Security/ Filesystem Security.

You need to set the recommended permissions for working with system files in the table. Sometimes, they change without the participation of the site administrator due to the routine work of hosting and when you install themes and plugins. You should visit this page regularly and set the permissions that are recommended here.

You need to activate the "*Disable PHP files editing*" checkbox. This will prevent damage to necessary files of plugins and themes. Mostly, we are talking about accidental changes to such files, but I want to warn you. Do not edit plugin files or theme files unless you are the author. It is important. I think you understand this yourself.

You need to activate the "*Prevent Access to default WP files*" checkbox. The fewer opportunities a site's visitors have to obtain any information about it, the better for site security.

On the same tab, activate the "Prevent hotlinking" switch. This will prevent scammers from inserting images stored on your server into publications on their websites.

On the "*Host system logs*" tab, you will be able to view system error logs if they occur. This can be very useful, but fortunately, such a need arises very rarely. If you do everything right and do not get carried away with risky experiments, then you may never see these logs in your life or see them empty.

If records appear there, they most often record fairly ordinary temporary failures during operations on the server.

In short, these logs are not a means of diagnosing or checking the quality of the site. They serve to find out the reasons if something goes wrong.

The "*WP Security/Blacklist Manager*" page (Figure 3-13) deserves serious attention. Here, using manual operations, we maintain lists of *IP* addresses and user agents that we have banned from visiting the site. This is the same permanent ban that everyone has heard about. ***Note: this feature is planned to be moved to the "WP Security/Firewall" page!***

Of course, this opportunity must be used carefully. We will discuss this in detail in the book, which will focus on website maintenance and support.

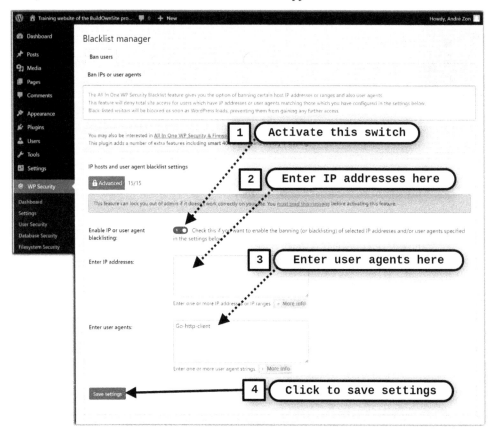

Figure 3-13. WP Security/ Blacklist Manager.

Now let's add the name *Go-http-client* to the list of blocked agents and click the "*Save settings*" button.

We now just protected the entire site from downloading using one of the most popular programs used for this.

The "*WP Security/ Firewall*" page (Figure 3-14) contains the settings for one of the key security components of the site. I'll go through all the tabs, and you'll see which features you should activate.

Of course, you can change these settings yourself in the future, but you should not touch the two tabs at all for now. You do not need to do anything on the "*404 Detection*" and "*Advanced Settings*" tabs. Please note: Each tab has its own button for saving settings.

On the "WP Security/ Firewall: Basic Firewall Rules" tab (Figure 3.14), activate switches in all blocks except "Disable WordPress RSS and ATOM feeds." If you want to hide RSS and ATOM feeds, you must also activate the switch in this block.

There are no specific recommendations on this matter.

Not many people use readers for RSS and ATOM formats, and this is mainly a technically advanced audience. These feeds can also be used for syndication with other sites.

There is no longer any benefit from them at present time, but there may be problems with indexing by search engines.

If you have a niche information site, disabling this option and getting 10 additional points towards the site's security level assessment is better.

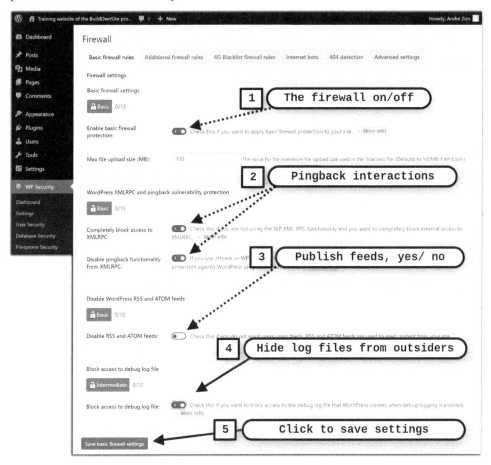

Figure 3-14. WP Security/ Firewall/: Basic Firewall Rules.

After activating all the switches on the tab, click the "Save basic firewall settings" button and go to the "Additional Firewall Rules" tab (Figure 3.15).

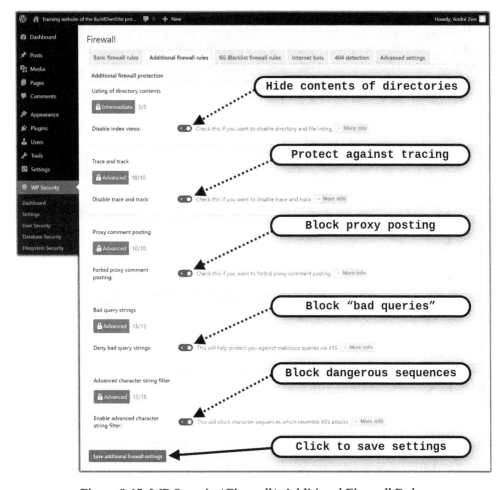

Figure 3-15. WP Security/ Firewall/: Additional Firewall Rules.

On this tab, activate all switches. Then click the "Save additional firewall settings" button and go to the "6G Blacklist firewall rules" tab (Figure 3.16).

On this tab, activate the switches in the topmost block "6G Blacklist/firewall settings". Then click the "Save 5G/ 6G firewall settings" button in this block and go to the "Internet bots" tab (Figure 3.17).

On this tab, activate the switches and click the "Save Internet bot settings" button.

We have finished setting up the firewall, and now we will look at the remaining pages of the plugin settings.

The "*WP Security/ Brute Force*" page contains everything you need to protect against website hacking using password guessing. We solve this problem by other means, and I do not recommend activating this component. It is best to start using it when you become more experienced. In inexperienced hands, this component can block access to the site, even for the administrator himself. Therefore, you don't need to do anything here for now.

We don't need the "*WP Security/ Spam Prevention*" page at all for now since we don't use commenting features. In the future, if you have such a need, you can use this page to improve protection against spam in comments. This is a very helpful addition to the standard commenting controls in *WordPress* itself. We have already studied them.

Figure 3-16. WP Security/ Firewall/: 6G Blacklist firewall rules.

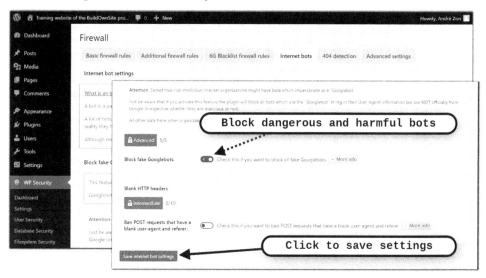

Figure 3-17. WP Security/ Firewall/: Internet bots.

The "*WP Security/ Scanner*" page does not require any mandatory settings. Here, you have access to tools to check the integrity of the system and the absence of foreign malicious codes. These checks are best done manually rather than automatically. In addition, we will install another scanner plugin. You will need to work with them at the stage of support and maintenance of a ready-made and running website. We will look at this issue in the book devoted to website maintenance.

The "*WP Security/Miscellaneous*" page (Figure 3-18) contains some pretty essential settings. Here, we can protect site pages from being simply copied to the clipboard using right-click content selection. Here, we can prevent our website content from being inserted into third-party pages. Here, we can prevent attempts by attackers to identify the authors of site publications. Here, we can block unauthorized access to the site's software. Just do it all (besides the "WP REST API" and "Salt").

Figure 3-18. WP Security/ Miscellaneous.

The site administrator will not feel these restrictions and can use the right mouse button on the site pages as usual.

The "*WP Security/ Tools*" page (Figure 3-19) contains another handy tools that are not directly related to site security. Using "Password Tool," you can quickly and easily generate strong passwords for use anywhere.

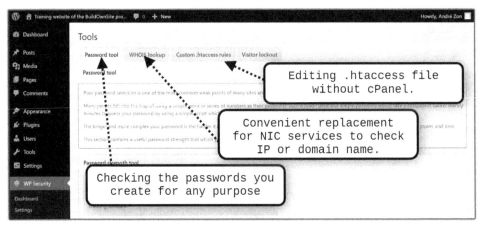

Figure 3-19. WP Security/ Tools.

Using "*WHOIS Lookup*," you can obtain information about the ownership of domain names and *IP* addresses. This will be very useful when you find out who exactly is trying to access the site or who owns the domain you are interested in. On the "Custom .htaccess rules" tab, you can create code snippets that the plugin will add directly to the .htaccess file.

For this purpose, using the already familiar combination of cPanel/ File Manager is still more reliable. The capabilities of the "Visitor lockout" tab seem redundant because WordPress does an excellent job of putting the site into a mode that blocks visitors when installing any updates. You might find this tab useful someday, but it's highly unlikely.

We will not consider the "Two Factor Auth" page. This feature usage is up to you. It's better not to use it for now so as not to lose access to your own site accidentally. In the future, if you have reasons to look for ways to make your WordPress login as secure as possible, you can take advantage of this opportunity. But don't forget to make a full backup of your site first!

So, we have considered all the issues related to this plugin and made all the necessary settings. Our site's security indicator shows 260 points (Figure 3-20). This is quite enough.

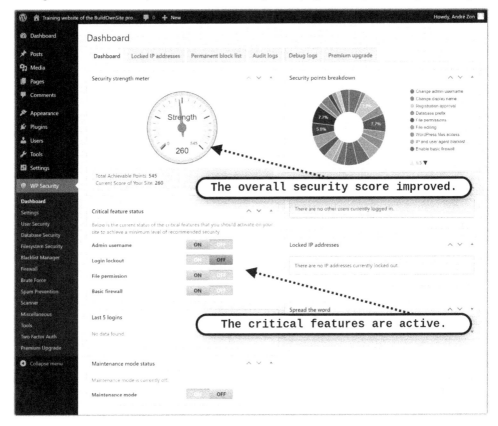

Figure 3-20. WP Security/ Dashboard page: final security score.

3.3.3. Disabling and Re-enabling the AIO WP Security plugin

The considered plugin significantly limits the ability to access the site's service data. Therefore, sometimes you may need to temporarily disable it, for example, to perform configuration operations for another plugin that requires full access to data.

The plugin is disabled in the usual way - by clicking the *Deactivate* link in the plugins table on the *Plugins* page.

When you disable a plugin, its settings will be reset. To avoid setting it up from scratch after re-activation, you need to save its settings in a file that will be automatically saved on the local hard drive of your computer. Then, you will restore the plugin settings from this file when necessary. It will only take a few seconds.

So, we need to open the *WP Security/ Settings* page and click the *Import/ Export* tab on it (Figure 3-21).

Then, you need to click the "*Export AIOS settings*" button in the block of the same name. The plugin will automatically generate a settings file and start downloading it to the *Downloads* folder on your hard drive. The file name will look like

```
aiowps_yyyy-mm-dd_hh-mm.txt
```

that is, it will contain the current date, hours, and minutes at the time of downloading.

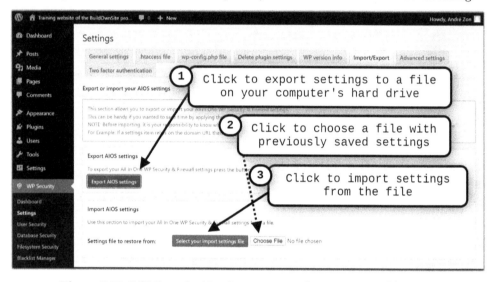

Figure 3-21. WP Security/ Settings page, settings export and import.

You can save different options for plugin settings in such files if you need different options for quickly configuring it. Rename them so that you can quickly navigate through the saved settings.

After performing operations that required disabling the plugin, you must reactivate it. To do this, click the *Activate* link in the plugins table on the *Plugins* page.

Then, you can load the desired settings file using the "*Choose File*" button in the "*Import AIOS settings*" block. Once the file is downloaded, you can instantly apply the settings saved in it. To do this, you must click the "*Select Your Import Settings File*" button in this block.

After re-activation, the *All On One WP Security & Firewall* plugin will offer you to automatically save and restore all settings during subsequent deactivations and activations.

When you see the message "*Would you like All In One WP Security & Firewall to restore the config settings and re-insert the security rules in your .htaccess file, which were cleared when you deactivated the plugin?*", just click the "*Yes*" button. And you will no longer need to import and export its settings.

Now, we need to install and configure another plugin responsible for security. It's called *NinjaFirewall*. This is an excellent addition to an already installed and configured plugin.

3.3.4. Plugin for Additional Protection Using a Firewall

Let's open the plugin installation page, find the *NinjaFirewall* plugin, and install and activate it.

This plugin adds its own line to the menu on the left sidebar. Below this line, there is a plugin submenu with several items.

To configure the plugin, we only need the *NinjaFirewall/ Firewall Policies* item. Here (Figure 3-22), you need to open the *Basic Policies* tab, then in the *Uploads* block, select the *Disallow Uploads* option, and activate all the checkboxes. After this, click the *Save Firewall Policies* button at the bottom of the page. After refreshing the page, you will see that two checkboxes in the *WordPress XML-RPC API* block have become inactive again. This is okay. The plugin is fairly intelligent; it checked your system configuration and deactivated redundant settings.

There is no need to make any further settings for this plugin.

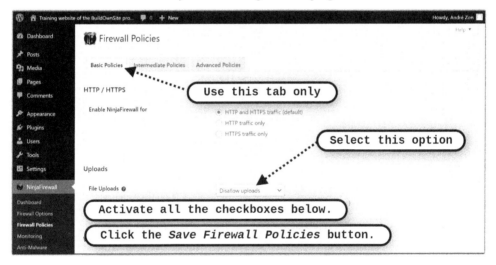

Figure 3-22. NinjaFirewall/ Firewall Policies.

Now, I will tell you why this plugin is actually needed. Firstly, it successfully complements the main *AIO WP Security* plugin we have already configured and does not conflict with it. Secondly, it creates an additional layer of protection. Thirdly, it has very important tools that are difficult to replace.

This plugin not only blocks dangerous and suspicious requests to the site. It keeps records of them in a particular journal. Therefore, you don't have to do the tedious work of analyzing server logs. If the site is working well, all you need to do is regularly check the log of this plugin and, if necessary, take additional measures to protect the site. We will discuss these measures in detail in the book devoted to website maintenance.

The log is available on the *NinjaFirewall/ Logs* page (Figure 3-23) under the *Firewall Log* tab. Now, this log is still empty, but it has already begun its work and will be updated constantly. A new log file is created every month, and you can always select the month that interests you.

The structure of the log is very simple.

Each line contains information about one suspicious or dangerous request and contains all the details about it. They will be very useful to us at the site maintenance and support stage.

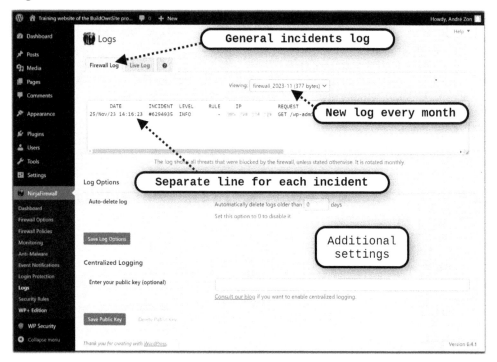

Figure 3-23. NinjaFirewall/ Logs/ Firewall Log.

But that's not all.

This plugin allows you to monitor the actions of site visitors in real-time mode!

Click on the *Live Log* tab (Figure 3-24). This log is currently disabled and can be enabled with the *Disabled* button. Once clicked, this button changes color to green and the text to *Enabled*.

If you click on it again, the real-time log will turn off. There is no need to leave the log turned on. This can cause your work files to become overcrowded and your site to slow down. Therefore, after studying real-time data, this log should be disabled.

Why is this necessary? This log is an incredibly convenient tool for quickly identifying, for example, an *IP* address from which many suspicious requests are coming. If *Google Analytics* real-time statistics show unusually high traffic, this could indicate an attack or an attempt to download your entire site.

In this case, you just need to open this log and look at the composition and nature of the requests and the addresses from which these requests are sent.

This can help if an attacker is actually sending the requests, or cancel the alarm if it simply turns out that a high-quality external link worked and interested visitors visited your site.

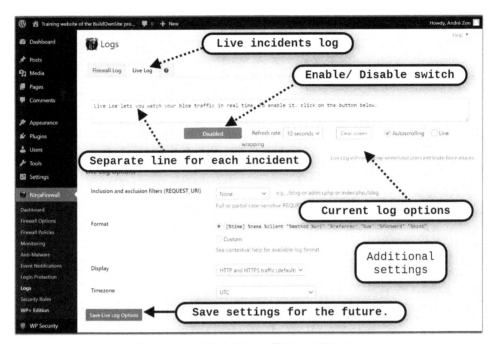

Figure 3-24. NinjaFirewall/ Logs/ Live Log.

With this plugin, you need to do some more steps to configure the alerts that it sends to email. This is done on the *NinjaFirewall/Event Notifications* page (Figure 3-25).

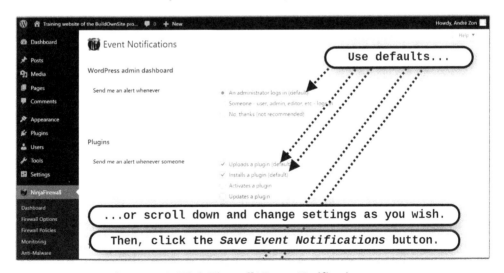

Figure 3-25. NinjaFirewall/ Event Notifications page.

This plugin sends email notifications about events that relate not only to security but also to changes in the site configuration and everything related to access attempts, including your own. This is very useful, and over time, you will decide which alerts you want to receive and which you don't. For now, everything can be left as is.

3.3.5. Additional WordPress File Verification Plugin

The *NinjaScanner* plugin is associated with the *NinjaFirewall* plugin. Let's install and activate it.

He also adds its own menu line to the left sidebar. This line does not contain a submenu and leads to the site scanning page (Figure 3-26). Here, you can check the integrity of service files and the presence of malicious codes.

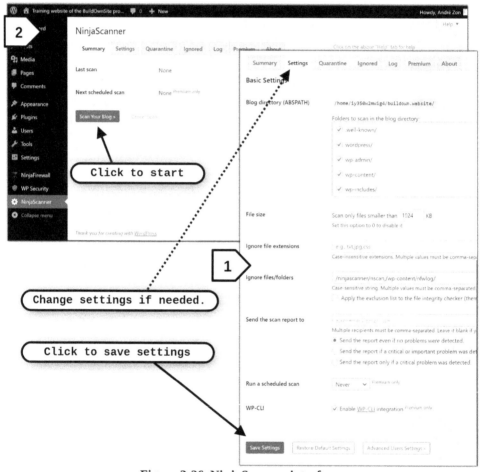

Figure 3-26. NinjaScanner interface.

You have already seen that similar tools are available in the *AIO WP Security plugin*. I recommend the *NinjaScanner* plugin as an additional tool for checking. It is associated and compatible with the *NinjaFirewall* plugin and forms a common feature space with it. Additional security features are rarely redundant, right?

With the installation of these plugins, we have completed creating a security system for our site.

Now, we need to solve one more problem in the interests of the security and authority of the site.

We will close the site to visitors.

3.4. Closing the Website to Visitors

This is a simple task and it won't require much effort.

It is best to use a specialized plugin for this. It does not directly affect the site's security system, is not related to security settings, and allows you to activate not only the *Coming Soon* mode while your site is not yet ready but also the *Maintenance Mode* if you need to perform some work urgently.

In addition, specialized plugins provide many possibilities for the visual design of pages that will be shown to site visitors. This can be very important, especially if you need to emphasize your brand or, for example, display a countdown.

I have tried various plugins that allow me to solve this problem. When writing this book, I used a plugin called "*Nifty Coming Soon & Maintenance Page*."

Let's open the plugin installation page, find the plugin, install it, and activate it. This plugin adds the "*Nifty Options*" item to the menu on the left sidebar. The site's home page will immediately be replaced by a page that replaces the site's home page.

You can choose the homepage's appearance on the "*Themes*" tab (Figure 3-27).

Figure 3-27. Nifty Coming Soon & Maintenance Page/ Nifty Options/ Themes.

I recommend not using the "*Customize*" option on the "*Welcome*" tab. This option deals with customizing the appearance of pages using a standard *WordPress* component that is typically used to customize themes. We haven't explored this tool yet, and it's too early to experiment with it.

Additionally, settings made for the temporary page may conflict with settings for some themes. This is not a drawback of the plugin. Rather, it is a consequence of its merits, which in most cases simply turns out to be unnecessary.

Of course, you can experiment with the settings in the "*Nifty Options*" page (Figure 3-28) if you so desire. It will most likely be safe. We haven't gotten around to installing and configuring themes yet, and conflicts are extremely unlikely.

Figure 3-28. Appearance/ Customize/ Nifty Options page.

In fact, the ready-made themes also look quite picturesque, but they are only available in the paid version of the plugin. It's a matter of taste and your choice.

By the way, while we were discussing all these details, we forgot to look at what the main page of the site looks like. We open it and see... that nothing happened. Is the plugin not working?

Everything is fine; the plugin works. It's just that you are logged in to the *WordPress* interface, and therefore, you see the site differently than it looks to a visitor. Pay attention to the top toolbar - and you will understand everything. We'll have to launch a different browser to see what the site's home page looks like. But the easiest way is to simply open a new *Google Chrome* window in *Incognito Mode*. As you can see, everything works fine. Why didn't we see this in the main browser window?

This happened because, according to generally accepted practice, all actions that limit the visibility of site pages or prohibit any operations with them do not apply to authorized personnel. Therefore, you can safely work with the site after you have closed it to visitors.

Just remember to check how your site looks to regular visitors using *Incognito* mode. Have you already guessed that the same thing happens when selecting text with the mouse? But we have already closed the site from visitors.

If you need to open the site's main page for some time to those who are not authorized, just deactivate the plugin. When you need to close it again, activate it.

After the official opening of the site and the start of indexing its content by search engines, you will no longer need this plugin, and it can be deleted or deactivated.

I can also recommend another plugin for closing the site from visitors, which has a very long name, "*Coming Soon Page, Maintenance Mode, Landing Pages & WordPress Website Builder by SeedProd.*" This plugin is somewhat easier to configure, but it is more flexible.

After installation, you need to activate the switch on the "*Coming Soon Mode*" block and click the "*Edit*" button on the same block (Figure 3-29). You don't have to do anything in the splash page editor; you just need to click the "*Save*" button on the right side of the top toolbar; otherwise, the splash page won't work.

Figure 3-29. Coming Soon Page/ Coming Soon Mode page.

You can check the splash screen in the same way as for the first plugin - open the site's main page in Incognito mode or simply use another computer.

Now, we need to install and configure plugins that are responsible for site speed and performance.

3.5. Installing and Configuring Performance Plugins

3.5.1. Backend Caching Plugin

As we have already seen in the site health results, it is recommended to install a caching plugin to improve site performance.

Such plugins, as we have already said, are able to store in finished form files of website pages that have already been opened in the browser. This allows you to avoid them being regenerated in a dynamic way, which, in turn, sharply reduces the period of time between the moment the page address is entered in the browser and the moment it appears on the screen.

At the same time, the number of calls to the database, *WordPress* core programs, theme components, and plugins is reduced. This allows you to reduce the consumption of server resources and reduce the load on its disk and processor. This means that your site will be able to process more requests and display more pages per unit of time. Your site will be able to handle very high traffic without you having to pay more for hosting.

There are many great caching plugins out there. Each of them has its own characteristics, and each solves various particular problems with varying degrees of effectiveness. In addition, the same plugin may work better under one host configuration and worse under another.

Before you begin installing and configuring the caching plugin, there are a few essential notes to make.

Installing a caching plugin for the backend is traditionally considered absolutely mandatory because it is simply impossible to do otherwise.

This is a wrong point of view.

It happens that a caching plugin consumes more resources than it saves. Therefore, keep in mind that usually, after launching a site, experienced bloggers and technically trained site owners check the site's performance indicators and server load with and without a caching plugin.

If the *Core Web Vitals* system indicators are in the "green zone" and the server load is quite far from the maximum possible, then it is better to do without a caching plugin. This usually happens if the site traffic is no more than several thousand visits per day.

Of course, if the traffic is large enough, and it amounts to at least tens of thousands of visits per day, and this creates a noticeable load on the server, then such a plugin becomes absolutely necessary.

There are quite a few caching plugins for *WordPress*, and the official repository on *wordpress.org* has plugins that have millions of downloads. This does not mean that they are all equally good in every situation.

Moreover, although any backend caching plugin potentially reduces the load on the server, you should always understand that this is not the only parameter that needs improvement.

If a caching plugin works well and quickly, but search engines have complaints about the quality and performance of site pages, then this may indicate that the caching plugin is not suitable for your site hosted on a specific host. In this case, the plugin will need to be replaced with another one.

It is best to focus on the recommendations of the support service and technical documentation of your hosting company.

In our case (at the time of writing this book), the web server is running the *LiteSpeed* operating system, so we will not do unnecessary searches and install a caching plugin that was created by this OS developers. If your server is running an OS different from LightSpeed, it's recommended to register in the QUIC.cloud CDN service (there is a free plan is available, look at ***https://www.quic.cloud/***).

This plugin works great with other operating systems, so you can safely use it on any hosting. It quickly became popular and received excellent reviews.

Let's install and activate the plugin. It adds its own menu to the left sidebar, which is accessible via the *LiteSpeed Cache* line.

This is one of the awesome plugins that works well out of the box without any additional settings. However, we will make one adjustment. Let's open the L*iteSpeed Cache/ Cache* page and go to the *Object* tab (Figure 3-30). Activate the "*Object Cache*" switch and click the "*Save Changes*" button.

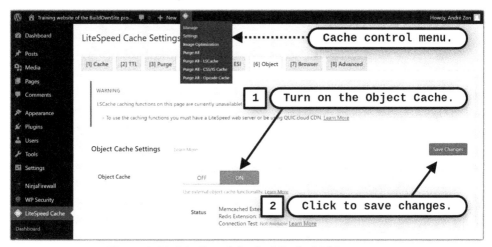

Figure 3-30. LiteSpeed Cache/ Cache/ Object page.

Ready. You don't need to do anything else to configure this plugin.

Look at the top toolbar.

An icon in the form of a diamond appeared on it. This is a link to the quick access menu to the settings and capabilities of the plugin and, most importantly, to several items whose names begin with the word "*Purge.*" These items activate the deletion of cache contents, which are generated and stored for quick transmission to the visitor's browser.

Why clear the cache memory? After all, this will immediately lead to a slowdown of the site and practically neutralize all the results of the caching plugin!

Yes, it will lead to a slowdown, but very briefly, because after the first access to any page of the site, its generated static version will already be in the cache, and then the same will happen to the remaining pages, and the site will start working quickly again.

Everything is straightforward. If you edit an already published post, or replace an illustration in it, or improve the design of the page, the site visitor will not notice it. It will still see the old "cached" version. To ensure that the contents of the cache are always up to date, it must be cleared periodically. Over time, you will get used to it.

By the way. The plugin itself also periodically clears the cache when, in its opinion, it is needed. Therefore, in the site management console, you will often see messages indicating that the cache was cleared successfully.

So, we are done with this plugin. As you probably already guessed, this plugin is responsible for the fast operation of the backend.

This is not the only caching plugin that we will need to install.

The popular *Autoptimize* plugin works very well in tandem with it. It allows you to solve some small but very important tasks related to the frontend - to reduce the load not on the server but on the browser of the site visitor. Now you will see this.

3.5.2. Frontend Caching Plugin

Let's find, install, and activate the *Autoptimize* plugin. This plugin does not add its own lines to the left sidebar menu of the system, so its settings are accessed through the "*Plugins/Installed Plugins*" page. In the table of installed plugins, find the *Autoptimize* plugin line and click the *Settings* link. This is actually the classic way to access plugin settings. Another one - via the left menu item Settings/ Autoptimize (Figure 3-31).

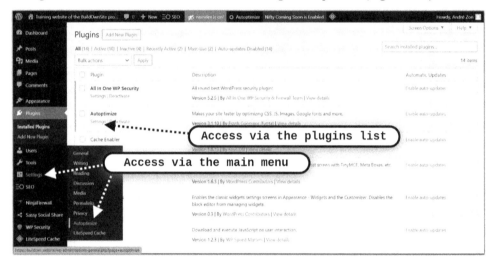

Figure 3-31. Ways to access Autoptimize/ Settings page.

The plugin settings page automatically opens in the "*JS, CSS & HTML*" tab.

On this page (Figure 3-32), you need to activate and deactivate some checkboxes. In fact, everything is straightforward here: you need to enable all settings blocks and activate all checkboxes, except those that are not recommended to be enabled. We will return to this issue in the next book when we deal with additional *SEO* optimization. Since this entire screenshot takes up too much space, we will list all the checkboxes to be activated in list form here. Please be careful when making settings as described above.

JavaScript Options: "*Optimize JavaScript Code?*", "*Do not aggregate but defer?*", "*Also defer inline JS?*".

CSS Options: "*Optimize CSS Code?*".

HTML Options: "*Optimize HTML Code?*".

Misc Options: All checkboxes.

All of the other checkboxes must be deactivated, and all of the editable strings must remain empty.

At the end of the job, click the "*Save Changes and Empty Cache*" button.

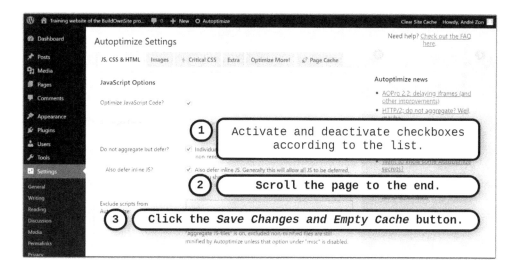

Figure 3-32. Autoptimize/ Settings/ JS, CSS & HTML page.

Then, you need to go to the *Extra* tab (Figure 3-33).

Activate the "*Remove emojis*" checkbox and the "*Remove query strings from static resources*" checkbox.

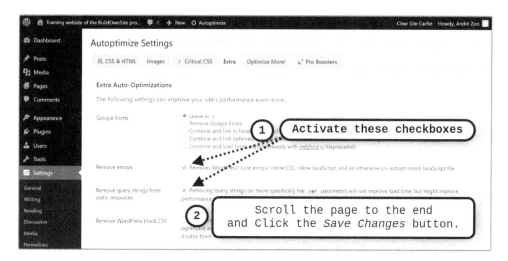

Figure 3-33. Autoptimize/ Settings/ Extra page.

Click the "*Save Changes*" button.

All is ready.

Pay attention to the top toolbar (Figure 3-34). The *Autoptimize* plugin added its link to it. When you click on it, you will be taken to the settings page, and when you hover your mouse, you will be able to see a drop-down window that contains information about the state of the cache and a link to the function to clear it.

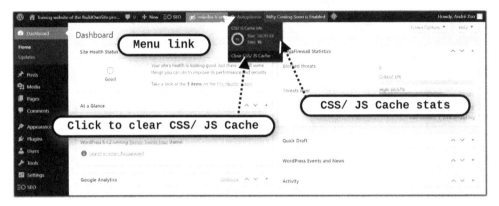

Figure 3-34. WordPress interface page with the Autoptimize toolbar.

You need to clear the *Autoptimize* cache when there are changes in the design of the site, as well as after adding and removing plugins, fragments, and widgets and changing the theme.

3.5.3. Additional Plugins to Increase Website Performance

Now install and activate two more plugins: *Flying Scripts* and *Lazy Load for Videos* (Figure 3-35). We won't set them up now; we'll come back to them in the advanced optimization and *SEO* phase of the next book, which is dedicated to content creation.

Figure 3-35. Plugin search pages with additional performance plugins.

The *Flying Scripts* plugin allows you to significantly improve site performance in the *Core Web Vitals* system by deferring the loading of individual *JS* code fragments, and the *Lazy Load for Videos* plugin allows you to defer the loading of videos published on *YouTube*.

The next important step is installing plugins that are designed to solve onsite *SEO* problems.

3.6. Installing and Configuring SEO Plugins

3.6.1. Choosing and Installing an SEO Plugin

Many different plugins for *WordPress* can be used to solve various problems in the interests of *SEO*. Some of these plugins are traditional leaders and enjoy deserved popularity. I have tested all the leaders of this group of plugins, and they are really excellent.

This group also includes the relatively little-known *SEO Press* plugin. I've been working with it on several projects for a few years now, and it has become a really great product over that time.

It would be correct to say a few words why I chose this particular plugin.

The *SEO* segment is one of the most commercialized among all *WordPress* plugin groups. This is easy to understand because successful *SEO* is vital for any website. And there are a lot of these tasks today!

Therefore, there are simply no completely free *SEO* plugins that could solve all of the *SEO* problems.

You can, of course, try to collect a collection of free plugins that would all be capable of this, but it's better not even to try. This creates too many risks and can lead to site crashes due to plugin incompatibility.

If we look at the functions that the most popular plugins are capable of performing, we will find that they are almost completely the same.

When choosing an *SEO* plugin, you need to take into account many factors that affect ease of use and the practicality of the choice in general. It is also vital that the free version of the plugin is powerful enough and capable of solving all the most important tasks without restrictions.

That is why, after many tests and checks, I chose the *SEO Press* plugin.

Its free version is very functional; the paid extension provides really valuable features. It works great, does not slow down the site, and has a convenient and straightforward interface.

When writing this book, the license for the paid version of this plugin allows you to use it on five sites simultaneously.

We will install the free version of the plugin first and then supplement it with the paid version. At the same time, you will learn how you can install the plugin using a different method than from the *WordPress* repository.

Install and activate the *SEO Press* plugin. The plugin adds a link to its menu in the left sidebar (Figure 3-36). The menu is quite extensive, even in the free version of the plugin.

If you decide to buy the professional version of the *SEO Press* plugin, then you need to do this on the plugin developer's website. This is standard practice because the *WordPress* depository only offers free versions and does not sell premium versions of plugins and themes.

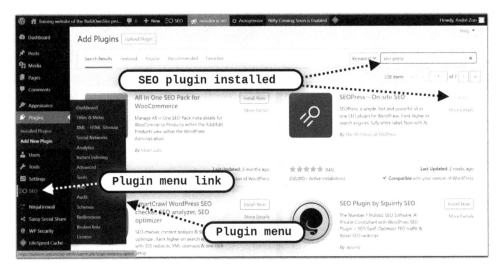

Figure 3-36. installed SEO Press plugin and the left sidebar menu.

The link to purchase the extended version of the plugin is on the SEO/ Dashboard page (Figure 3-37).

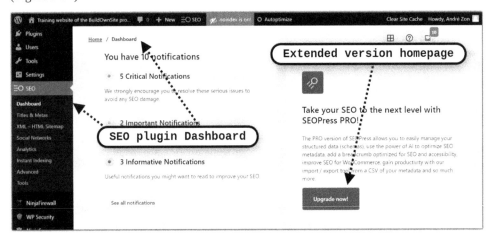

Figure 3-37. SEO Press plugin and link to its PRO version.

3.6.2. How to Install the Extended Version of the Plugin

The extended version of the plugin is distributed as a downloadable archive; this is standard practice.

You can download the archive using the link after registration and payment on the developer's website, on the *Downloads* page in the account that you will have to create on the developer's website, or via the link in the letter confirming the purchase.

To install the extended version, you need to open the *Plugins/ Add New* page and click the *Upload Plugin* button. The system will display a hint about the order of plug-in installation, under which there will be a *Choose File* button.

In the download window, you need to select the archive file with the extended version of the plugin and click the *Open* button (Figure 3-38). The plugin will be uploaded to the system and installed immediately.

Figure 3-38. Installing the SEO Press PRO plugin from the archive.

After this, you will need to obtain a *License Key* from the developer's website. To do this, you need to log into your account, open the *My License Keys/ Subscriptions* page, and copy the *License Key* code. Write it to a temporary file or directly to Planner.

Then you need to open the *Plugins/ SEO Press PRO/ License* page (Figure 3-39), enter the license code in the *License Key* field, click the *Save Changes* button, and then *Activate License.* Ready. Now, you can use all the features to solve your *SEO* problems. The extended version of the plugin does not create its own link on the left sidebar of the system but adds new items to the menu that was created when installing the free version and complements the pages and settings of the free version.

We don't need other plugins to solve *SEO* problems now, and it's unlikely that such a need will arise in the future.

We will perform basic *SEO* settings now, and we will use advanced features when filling the site with content, as described in the next book in the series.

3.6.3. SEO Plugin Setup

Many of the plugin's features are already configured out of the box; we'll just clarify some items. Open the *SEO/Dashboard* page (Figure 3-40). Since this entire screenshot takes up too much space, we will list all the switches to be activated or deactivated in list form here. There is a button here that takes you to a collection of video tutorials for users. Be sure to take the time to study them.

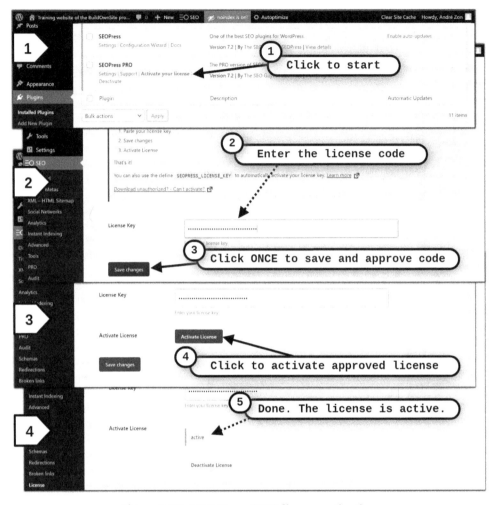

Figure 3-39. SEO Press PRO license activation.

We are interested in the *SEO Management* block. Here, you can enable entire groups of functions and settings. Look at their list. For the simple informational site we are creating, we don't need "*Local Business*," "*WooCommerce*," "*Easy Digital Downloads*," and "*Google News Sitemap*."

Also, we don't need the "*URL Rewriting*" feature because we solved the issue with the permalink structure during the *WordPress* setup stage. If, in some cases, you need this feature, you can activate it and change the permalinks according to your tasks and needs using this plugin. You will not need to change your *WordPress* permalink settings.

We disable these features and enable all others.

Let me explain a little about the possibilities that we are not currently using.

"*Local Business*" is everything that concerns the necessary settings and meta tags if you are creating a website for a real office, production, store, restaurant, and, in general, any company that exists not only as a website. This is very important for full integration with *Google My Business* and *Google Maps* services.

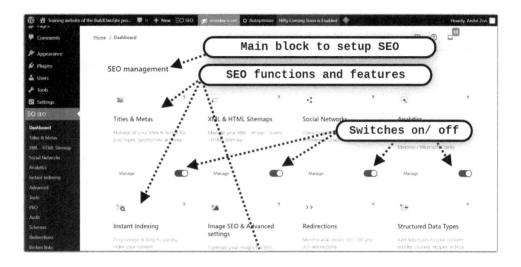

Figure 3-40. SEO/Dashboard page.

"WooCommerce" is everything that exists for *SEO* optimization of product descriptions when creating your own full-fledged online store. *WooCommerce* is the name of a specialized *WordPress* plugin that allows you to fully and efficiently solve all the tasks of creating and operating an online store. Now, this is not even just a plugin but a complex solution for which many different components have been developed. In terms of complexity, it is comparable to the entire *WordPress* system. If you plan to engage in sales, then after creating a website, you will need to study its capabilities further.

"Easy Digital Downloads" is a very popular solution for sales based on the plugin of the same name. Unlike *WooCommerce*, this solution only works with digital products.

"Google News Sitemap" is precisely what the name says. The *Google* search engine can broadcast your site's publications in its news feeds. But this is a matter of separate consideration and study. Only you can decide in the future whether your site will publish posts that may be considered news by *Google's* search engine. We will return to this issue in books on content creation and website promotion.

Now, you must hide the addresses of pages and publications from search bots. To do this, on the same page, deactivate the *XML&HTML Sitemaps* switch.

The same operation can be performed on the *SEO/ XML - HTML Sitemap* page. Here, you must deactivate the topmost main switch and click the *"Save Changes"* button.

We will perform some simple but essential settings when preparing the site for opening.

To complete the site configuration, we need to install a few useful plugins. At the content creation stage, we will need a few more plugins.

3.7. Installing Other Recommended Plugins

We will install a few more plugins to start working on the site content and provide some additional useful features.

Before we begin, there is one important note to make.

Recently, the *WordPress* system has been actively supplemented and developed through block design and block editing tools. Undoubtedly, such opportunities arise because they are dictated by demand.

There is also no doubt that almost all novice *WordPress* users are inspired by the new features that provide unprecedented flexibility in customizing everything imaginable on the sites.

Users with significant experience have treated and continue to treat these opportunities cautiously.

As a user with more than significant experience, I can give you very practical advice.

Don't use block design or block editing tools until you are a fairly experienced *WordPress* user.

If you persist in your desire to express your creative potential, then know that there is no surer way to drive a project into a dead end than creative work on its unique appearance. Experienced developers know this well.

That is why the most popular plugins, starting with version 6.0 of the *WordPress* system, include the *Classic Editor* and *Classic Widgets* plugins.

Also, keep in mind that classic *WordPress* themes were created by professionals who have gone through various stages of creative exploration and put a lot of conscious effort into creating themes. They understood what they were doing, knew how to do it, and had experience.

Therefore, it is best to start with ready-made classic themes and ready-made classic methods for working with content. You will have many ways to realize your creative potential in the future.

Now, you are faced with another task: creating a website as quickly as possible that will be perfect enough to compete on equal terms with those who have been on the market for a long time.

Let's install the *Classic Editor* and *Classic Widgets* plugins (Figure 3-41). They not only allow you to get started with simple operations quickly. They make it possible not to depend on the imagination and whims of developers of block themes and plugins. They are easier to use and give full control over the actions performed; for us now, this is the most important thing.

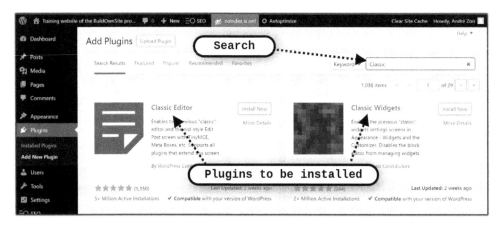

Figure 3-41. Search results for plugins with the word "Classic."

Both of these plugins require no configuration, do not add lines to the left sidebar, and do not slow down the site.

Radio buttons have been added to the *Settings/ Writing* page that allow you to set the Classic Editor as the default editor and allow or disable switching between the Block Editor and the Classic Editor.

Install them as you wish.

As you work, you will independently determine which option is more convenient for you.

We will focus on using the Classic Editor and describe the Block Editor's capabilities so that you can subsequently use any of them. Therefore, when creating your first website, it will be easier for you to use plugins rather than blocks to solve specific problems. You will make the final choice independently and consciously when your first website is completely ready.

So, we also need these plugins:

* *LuckyWP Table of Contents* or *Easy Table of Contents* - for adding tables of contents to posts,
* *WP Last Modified Info* - to add a line with the date of the last modification to posts,
* *WPFront Scroll Top* - for adding a button to rewind to the top of the page to the site pages,
* *Sassy Social Share* - for adding social sharing buttons to posts.

Adding a table of contents to your posts is very important for *SEO*. The fact is that search engines treat long posts well.

In order for such posts to effectively retain visitors, the text needs to be structured and its summary is shown at the top of the page.

In addition, the headings at various levels should contain the keywords of the post. This is taken into account by search engines when indexing.

The table of contents management plugin allows you to solve all these problems together.

The date of the last modification, which is displayed at the top of the post, is an important signal to the visitor. In fact, no one will want to read an old publication. And search engines give preference to sites where publications are regularly updated. Therefore, regularly updating posts and displaying the date of the last update is good for both *SEO* and user experience.

Scrolling to the top of the page improves the comfort of visitors reading long posts, especially when they are using mobile phones. Therefore, if the theme you choose does not have a built-in page rewind button, such a plugin will be very useful.

Traditional buttons, with which a site visitor can save a link to a post on a social network, send it using a messenger, publish it in a bookmarking service, or send it by mail, are actually a mandatory element of any site. To solve this problem, a stable, very fast, simple, and powerful plugin was chosen, even in the free version.

All these plugins are quite clear, visual, and self-documenting. We won't waste time studying them now.

In the end, over time, you can find a replacement for each of them, which may be more suitable for your site.

In the process of further work, we will, of course, take a closer look at the capabilities of these plugins.

In the meantime, we are finishing this stage of work on creating the site.

Stage Results

At this stage, we have completed a lot of very important work.

We have taken measures to protect the site from attackers on the server side, made the administrator account less vulnerable, and installed and configured plugins that guarantee the site a high level of security and allow you to control visitors' activity even in real-time.

We learned to close the site from visitors and closed it until it was ready to receive them.

We have installed and configured plugins that increase the site's speed and improve the measured parameters of the site's performance.

We have installed and configured plugins that allow you to solve all problems in the interests of *SEO*.

We have installed the necessary plugins to quickly start creating website content, improving user experience, and republishing posts on social networks, instant messengers, and social bookmarking services.

Now, our site can do everything necessary to start real work.

I hope you have recorded all the stage results in the Planner.

We have one more exciting stage ahead before we begin filling the site with content. We will install a *WordPress* theme on the site, customize it, and achieve the page design we need.

4

Customizing the Appearance of the WordPress Website

Stage Tasks

We are starting the fourth, very interesting stage of work on the site. Our site does not have a face yet. We have to create a face for it.

Before starting this work, you need to know and agree that website design is more about working on its internal structure and not on decor elements. If you don't get involved in the traditional debate about design and technology, then you can very briefly formulate the task of the stage.

We need to ensure that the site's appearance is precisely consistent with its composition, structure, content, functions, and purpose and is also attractive, or at least positively neutral, from the point of view of the average visitor representing the target audience.

Remember the visitor!

If you personally or your loved ones and friends like the way the site looks, this does not guarantee that visitors will like it, too. It is possible that the visitor is utterly indifferent to what shade of purple you used for the logo. The visitor solves his problems and achieves his goals.

Your task is to make sure that the site is liked, convenient, and valuable by the absolute majority of the potential target audience. Everything else is absolutely unimportant.

In cases of doubt, when you are unsure of the decisions made, it is best to seek advice from a specialist or experienced *WordPress* user. If there are no such people among your friends, then it's time for you to find thematic groups and communities on social networks. They will be happy to give you advice on any issue. Even if this advice is not the best and not the kindest, it will definitely be useful.

When your site is built on *WordPress*, your chosen theme is primarily responsible for the site's appearance. We discussed what a theme is in some detail in the first volume of the series, the book "*WordPress Website Building 101*".

Choosing a theme is very different from choosing a plugin, and you'll have to understand the difference first. We will form a list of basic requirements for the future theme, and I will tell you how you can check whether the theme meets them or not.

We will install one of the popular modern themes on the site, which uses both classic and block technologies.

We will actually be working with a child theme; this is a good practice that is definitely worth mastering.

A child theme is a theme that is created based on the one we chose. We will learn why you need to create a child theme, create it, and install it on the site.

We will study the theme settings system, find out their purpose, and use those we need at this stage.

Then, I will tell you how you can change the site's appearance using special codes - style sheets.

We'll then temporarily install a simple "classic" theme that doesn't use block technology.

Using an installed theme as an example, we will explore the possibilities for customizing it and the basic techniques for working with classic widgets. After this, we will return to the child theme we created and will continue to work only with it.

Finally, we will test the functionality and appearance of the site and find out how it will look on devices of different types.

We will make the final adjustments to the site's appearance and add the necessary visual elements after adding content - in preparation for the opening of a wholly finished site. How to do this will be described in the next book.

4.1. Classic WordPress Themes vs Block Themes

This is a good time to say something specific about block themes. There are very few of them on the official *WordPress* website compared to classic plug-and-play themes. At the end of 2022, there were only about 200 of them. In the fall of 2023, there were 450 of them. Of course, there is growth, but it is not a boom.

If you look at the installation statistics for block themes, it doesn't make a very good impression. The number of installations is in the tens, less often in the hundreds, and very rarely in the thousands. Histograms of block theme downloads often show a downward trend rather than an upward trend.

What's the matter?

After all, a block theme is a great way to customize a site and get a unique look for pages, as if the design was made specifically for the site.

This is something that falls on one side of the scale. At the same time, we should not forget that the design of even something as simple to use as a block layout of a single page is best handled by a professional designer. Otherwise, it will be difficult to achieve anything else besides uniqueness.

There are several reasons. They are on the other side of the scale.

First of all, working with a block design will not guarantee you the result you imagined even if you have great color sketches. It may well turn out that some of the creative ideas will not be realized due to some annoying technical banality. And you will have to adjust your vision and redo part of the work or even all the work.

Experienced web designers are well aware of the existence of such a trap since ancient times and can tell you many stories about clashes between the customer's creative imagination and crude technical reality. This point is specifically about fantasy and reality.

Secondly, working with blocks does not increase the designer's creative freedom but, on the contrary, limits it, oddly enough. A professional who develops a classic-type theme has the most creative freedom. It has fewer limitations, and therefore, any good classic theme will always look, on average, more professional and high-quality than a blocky one customized with your own hands.

Third, most block themes are only fast when they look like an empty box. As soon as you start filling it with blocks, the site slows down quickly and inexorably. This is due to the technical features of the block implementation.

For example, it is common practice for each block type to be accompanied by its own *CSS* file, which contains style descriptions for all block elements.

If, for a classic theme, you need to download from one to several such files, then for a block theme, there can be dozens of them. We won't go into detail any further; remember that most block-filled block themes are very, very slow.

A few more arguments could be put into this balance, but we'll stop for now. I think you already understand what we are talking about.

Block themes and block technologies for creating publications evoke an understandable surge of enthusiasm in novice webmasters and an irresistible desire to create a masterpiece. Imagine, or remember, the emotions of a child who was given a sketchbook for the first time, a large box of colored pencils, beautiful brushes, and a set of excellent watercolor paints. The emotions are incredible!

However, the child does not know how to draw, and no one taught him this properly. Therefore, interest in the gift quickly disappears in a matter of hours, and creative work ends with stained and warped sheets of paper, scattered pencils, dirty brushes, and soggy paints.

What do parents do in such cases?

If the child is upset, they console him and say that all this will be useful to him when he grows up a little and learns to draw better with felt-tip pens.

If the child is not upset, they don't say anything at all.

In both cases, they carefully collect all these beautiful pencils, brushes, and paints, put them in order, and put them in a box.

It's about the same story here.

There is nothing wrong with block technology, and in some cases, it can undoubtedly be irreplaceable. But it is just beginning its journey, and even the editor of the first *WordPress* block theme *Twenty Twenty-Three* is marked "beta."

However, the technology has appeared and already has fans and supporters. Excellent builders have already been developed, and very modern and prosperous themes have been created.

This technology definitely has a future.

You need to understand the difference between block technology for themes and block technology for posts.

Customizing a block theme can only be done using a special theme Block Editor.

Editing a publication can be done using the Classic Editor, or the Block Editor, or even combining their capabilities. I'll show you how this is done when we'll populate the site with content.

For now, let's get back to choosing a theme.

For us, the best way to get started and get the job done as quickly as possible is to choose a classic theme. If it also has block elements, so much the better, it will be easier to make comparisons.

You will always have time to return to experiments and working with block themes.

4.2. Choosing a WordPress Theme

4.2.1. Difficulties in Choosing a Theme

It's very simple to say: choose the suitable theme for your *WordPress* site. Making such a choice is quite tricky, especially for a beginner.

At the end of 2022, there were more than 10,000 themes in the official *WordPress* repository alone, and in the fall of 2023, their number exceeded 11,000!

But there are other depositories that specialize in selling paid themes, and there are thousands of them, too! Even if some themes are present in several places at once, there are still a lot of different themes.

This means that we need to have a system of criteria that will allow us to competently and quickly select a suitable theme.

Many novice creators of their own websites begin solving this issue by searching for reviews of the best, the fastest, the most beautiful, or the highest quality and, at the same time free themes. Of course, the search is done using the *Google* search engine.

Of course, there are a lot of such reviews. Most of them - those in the top search results - are either biased by hosting companies, sellers, and theme developers or are simply repeatedly rewritten and remade compilations of similar reviews. Most often, these reviews describe several dozen of the same themes.

To get a general idea of the themes, such overviews are pretty helpful. However, choosing a theme for your website based solely on information from such reviews is a somewhat risky decision. Although, in many cases, such a choice can save a lot of time - if among the popular themes you come across one that is suitable for your site, then why not choose such a theme?

Choosing a theme from the official *WordPress* repository can be very useful, too. There are a lot of real gems out there about which there are surprisingly few publications.

So, where to start?

4.2.2. Sequence and Criteria for Choosing a Theme

The smartest thing to do is to start by assigning a theme, keeping in mind your intention to choose between the free option and your willingness to pay the developer money, sometimes quite significant.

I think you should definitely pay money if you are making a commercial website and need functionality, quality, and a "white label." In this case, you will want a theme that, in the free version, will allow you to test the basic features and, in the full version, will allow you to solve all the tasks.

If you're making a personal blog and are only happy with a free theme, stick with that "free" strategy.

There are many great free themes out there. Many of them are related to donationware, and I am happy to pay their authors if the theme suits me.

The *WordPress* official website (***https://wordpress.org***) has a convenient and straightforward filter system with which you can easily navigate the proposed themes.

Here's what you need to pay attention to.

Carefully look at the list of themes selected using filters (Figure 4-1). Screenshots allow you to quite accurately and quickly understand the main thing - whether the theme is similar to what you are going to find.

Carefully read the summary and list of tags under the screenshot of the theme. Make sure the theme description matches your needs.

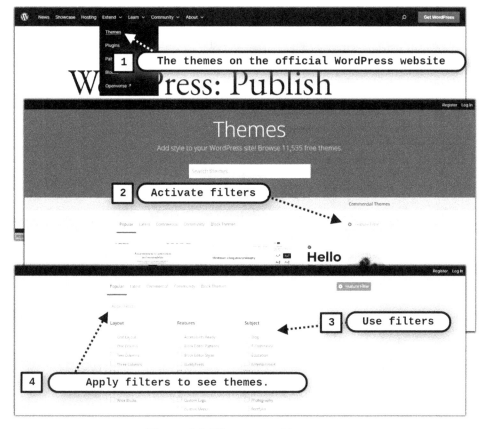

Figure 4-1. Theme searching pages.

Make a shortlist of themes. Each of these themes needs to be checked before installation on the site according to several criteria:

- date of last update,
- total number of installations,
- total number of reviews,
- share of negative reviews,
- the meaning and content of negative reviews,
- the presence of unresolved problems in the support forum,
- dynamics of the number of installations (growth or decline).

After such a check, your shortlist will probably become shorter. The themes that remain in it need to be checked using their "live demo", which exists for every theme worthy of attention.

We are primarily interested in the site's speed, which is built on the theme we need. It is the speed, as well as other parameters that are important from *Google's* point of view, that we need to check.

Here's how to do it (Figure 4-2).

4.2.3. Preliminary Check of Selected Themes

Open the page of your chosen theme on the official *WordPress* website (*https://wordpress.org*).

Of course, first you need to check all the points we just talked about. Then you need to go to the "*Theme Homepage*" link.

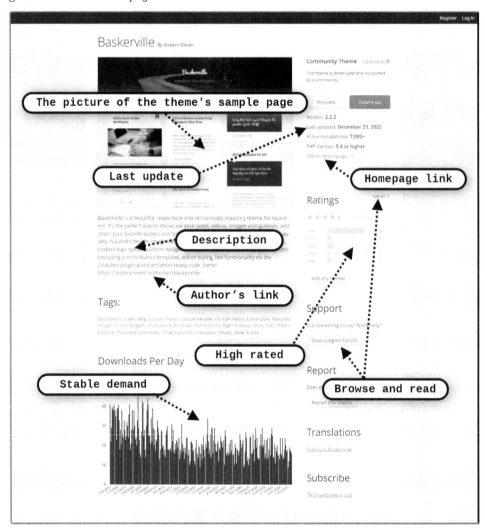

Figure 4-2. Chosen theme page.

We will be taken to the website of the theme developer, and on this website we will find a link to a demo site built on this theme.

Please note: large theme developers offer not only the themes themselves, but also specialized website templates built on them. Very often there are dozens of such templates, somewhat less often - hundreds.

Perhaps you will find what you need among them.

The common practice in such cases is that the theme itself with incomplete functionality is offered for free, while full functionality and ready-made website templates are only available for a fee. Some developers also offer free templates that are quite suitable for creating websites.

This is such a theme we will start with. This is a very famous and popular theme. Ready-made templates on the developer's website are grouped by purpose and topic. Paid template options are easy to distinguish from free ones.

Another important thing is that this theme is not entirely block-based. It successfully combines the ease of operation "out of the box" of a classic plug-and-play theme and the flexible customization elements inherent in block themes.

There are quite a lot of such "combined" themes, and today, they are, in most cases, the most practical and exciting.

So, we found the desired theme, went to its page, found a template that was interesting to us, opened its page, and clicked on the "*Demo*" button. We see in front of us the main page of the demo site.

You're probably thinking - why check it? Surely the developer tried to make sure that all its parameters were in "green circles"?

You will be surprised, but this is not so. Even for very large developers, this approach seems to be the exception, not the rule. Once you check out enough demo sites yourself, you will see this.

But at the top, developers sometimes show a very useful toolbar, with which you can see how the theme looks on various types of devices. Typically, this is a computer, a tablet in horizontal and vertical positions, and a phone in horizontal and vertical positions.

We can check this feature by clicking on the device icons (Figure 4-3). When you see the difference between how the same page looks on a computer screen and on a phone screen, remember that we'll talk about that in a bit.

Now, we need to understand the principle, and providing such an opportunity gives respect to the theme developer.

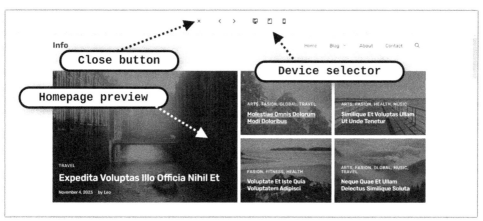

Figure 4-3. Theme homepage sample with a switch of device type.

The theme turned out to be responsive; it suited us, and we checked the speed and quality of its work using the *Lighthouse* plugin. And it turns out that there is only one green circle (Figure 4-4). What's the matter? Is the developer really selling a low-quality product?

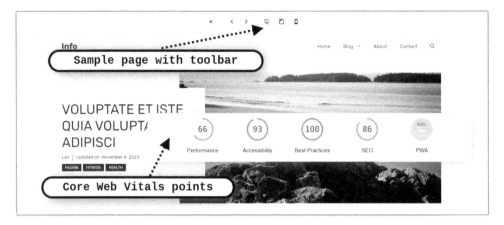

Figure 4-4. Core Web Vitals score for the demo page with the toolbar.

No. It is the toolbar with device icons that hinders an objective assessment. After all, it is not part of the future site! We need to get rid of him. Fortunately, the developer has provided the ability to hide it. Remove the toolbar from the screen and repeat the check.

As we can see, the picture immediately became better (Figure 4-5). And if you open the page of a separate post, the indicators will improve even more, usually in Performance.

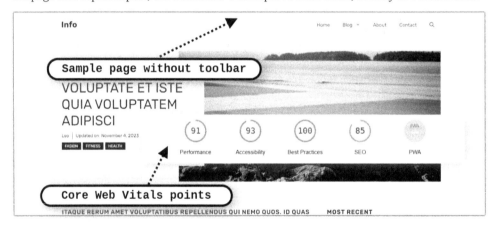

Figure 4-5. Core Web Vitals score for the demo page without the toolbar.

Advice for the future: if the developer has not provided the ability to hide the verification toolbar with device icons, you just need to click on any post on the demo site, and it will open in a window without a toolbar. After this, you can return to the main page of the demo site using the link that usually accompanies the logo, and there will still be no toolbar. Most often, this works.

At the same time, you can check the quality and speed parameters not only for the main page of the demo site but also for the post page. The home page is usually the slowest on any website.

As a result of the check, you can choose the theme that suits you and the template, if any. If you are unsure about the right choice, just choose a fast, multi-purpose theme.

We will work with the *Neve* theme, the free version. It is fast and has a lot of customization options. This theme has its own Block Editor that is relatively easy to use.

Once we're done with the *Neve* theme, I want you to understand what working with the classic theme looks like. When working with this theme, we will also use the capabilities of the *Classic Widgets* plugin.

You will be able to see and understand the main capabilities and differences between classic and block design. In the future, this will undoubtedly help you quickly and easily master the latest themes in the theme market.

Then, we will return to the *Neve* theme, or more precisely, a child theme based on it, and continue working with it.

4.3. Installing the Theme

Installing the theme is a straightforward process, and this chapter will be short. I highlighted this process as a separate one to slightly interrupt the discussions about the types and features of various themes.

It's just that before installing themes, we need to talk about a few important things that directly relate to the themes and deserve a separate, albeit short, discussion.

4.3.1. The Truth About Using Themes on Desktop and Mobile

When we discussed the various aspects of choosing a theme and touched on the issue of testing the appearance of pages on different types of devices, I suggested that you think about mobile devices.

The meaning of such thinking is quite simple, but very often, it eludes even quite experienced website owners. Everyone, of course, understands that a modern theme must be responsive; this is not even discussed. Once the test shows that on mobile devices, the theme obediently changes the appearance of the pages so that they successfully fit on the screen, this issue is considered resolved.

But at the same time, the choice of theme is still made on a regular desktop. The colors, shape of buttons, location of windows and widgets, column width, header and footer height, and much more are subject to the closest scrutiny.

But there is almost nothing of this on the phone screen! There is a simple color scheme, and texts, illustrations, and everything else are placed in one column. All the themes on the phone screen are incredibly similar, sometimes to the point of almost complete identity.

The thing is that the phone has become the main platform for website visitors. According to various estimates, the share of mobile users when browsing websites has exceeded 70 percent. At the same time, for sites with entertainment content, lifestyle, beauty, and cooking, mobile users account for more than 90 percent! If the site's topic is professional, then we can talk about 60-80 percent of mobile users and 20-40 percent of tablet and computer users.

This means that when choosing a theme for a website, you need to keep in mind its thematic matter. This pun has a very big practical meaning. In any case, the mobile platform is a priority today. This gives rise to many contradictions that deserve a separate discussion.

But for us, the conclusion is simple: before installing a theme, you need to very carefully not only check whether the site pages fit on the phone screen but also be very careful about checking their functioning.

Nowadays, there are quite a few themes aimed exclusively at mobile users. The rough black outlines of windows and buttons and heavy black fonts easily recognize them. They are the antipodes of glamorous themes that are still fashionable among beauty bloggers. Such glamour themes are designed for desktops; they have muted colors, small fonts, and colored pale backgrounds.

You need instead to focus on themes that provide compromise solutions. But on a phone screen, the font should be easy to read. The soft contrast between the background and the text must be sacrificed so that the *Lighthouse* tester doesn't tell *Google's* search engine that your site is hard to read.

One more note that directly concerns the connection between the operation of the site and the theme that you install on it.

Some very popular themes that offer a huge selection of ready-made website templates and fantastic customization options using block technology can lead to conflicts on the site. This also applies to classic-type themes. This picture is constantly changing, and I cannot say for sure which themes should be avoided and which themes are completely safe.

4.3.2. Themes' Safety

That's what is the problem. All the themes you install introduce a massive number of changes to the site configuration. But not all themes you delete remove everything after you. It also happens that your site is affected by components of an installed but inactive theme.

This can and sometimes does lead to the fact that when you change the theme and try to customize it, you may not get the result that it should be. Somewhere, the symbols have shifted, unnecessary indentations have appeared, and somewhere, elements have been stuck together that, in reality, have nothing in common. There are many options that are equally unpleasant and equally undesirable.

How to avoid this problem? Very simple. Before installing a new theme, be sure to completely back up the site - all its directories, files, and database. In the book about website technical support, we will consider this issue in as much detail as possible.

If something goes wrong, then you can simply delete your entire website with a hopelessly damaged design, and restore its previous version from a backup copy. All this will take a few minutes. In the meantime, we will work with a proven theme on our training site, which, frankly, is not scary.

4.3.3. How to Install a Theme

You need to open on your website the *Appearance/Themes* page and click the *Add New* button. You will see exactly the same results as on the official *WordPress* website. We have decided on a training theme, so you just need to enter its name in the search bar. The theme we need will come first.

By the way. Did you notice the *Upload Theme* button at the top of the page? This button opens a dialog for uploading a theme from the archive. Just like uploading paid versions of plugins, this option is needed to upload and install premium versions of themes. We won't do this now, but remember this opportunity for the future. Here, you can install a downloaded paid version of the theme whenever you need it.

To install the theme, place your mouse pointer over the thumbnail and click the Install button (Figure 4-6). The installation will begin immediately.

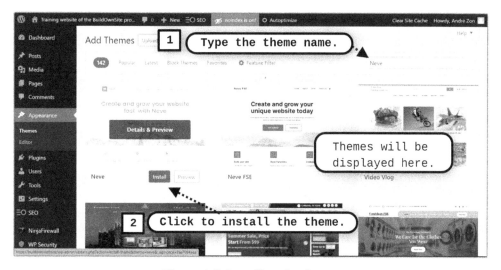

Figure 4-6. Installing the theme.

Once the theme installation is complete, we click the *Activate* button (Figure 4-7). The system will update the current site theme and automatically clear the cache. Look at the homepage of the site (Figure 4-8). The appearance has changed!

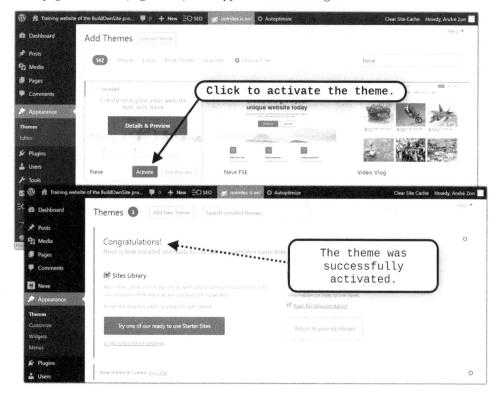

Figure 4-7. Activating the theme.

The site doesn't look very impressive because it has no content. No texts, no illustrations, no logo, no menu system.

It has nothing!

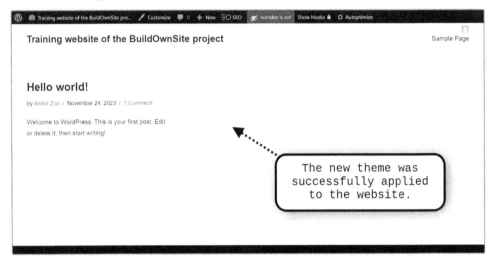

Figure 4-8. The new look of the empty homepage of the website.

To add content for debugging, you can use photos from your own phone. Our site is still closed to visitors, and no one will see anything yet.

When we get to creating content, I'll explain to you why you can't take photos from your phone without editing them.

You can also add a text placeholder if there are no ready-made texts. Just type "lorem ipsum" in *Google* search, and you will find an excellent text generator.

That's exactly what I did. I made several posts and added illustrations to them. Look, the site immediately changed and became similar to the real one (Figure 4-9).

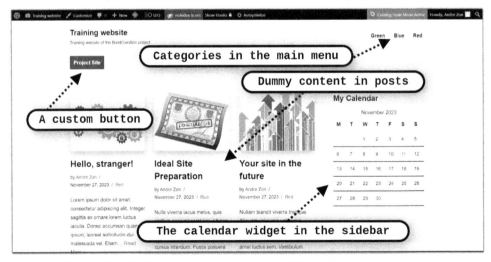

Figure 4-9. The homepage of the website filled with dummy content.

That's why I did it.

While there is no content on the site, we will not be able to evaluate the results of changing the theme settings. Some template elements, such as page numbers, will not be visible at all.

Until we customize the theme, we won't be able to evaluate the appearance of our actual content on the actual pages of the site.

To overcome this contradiction, I used dummy text and randomly selected images. By the way, I took legally free images from a public free collection.

Never use copyrighted content unless you have purchased a license for it!

As you add content to your own site, you'll come back to customizing the theme many times.

Before moving on to the settings, let's create and work with a child theme.

4.4. Creating the Child Theme

4.4.1. Why Do You Need a Child Theme?

A child theme is a simple and effective solution to multiple tasks simultaneously.

A child theme is a theme that is created based on the original parent theme, retains its appearance, performs all its functions, and has exactly the same settings system.

The most important thing is that all settings and changes that can be made in the child theme will remain untouched when updating the parent theme. In this case, all updates to the parent theme will appear in the child theme, too.

Updates to the parent theme and customizations to the child theme simply feed into each other and complement each other.

Using a child theme, you can add additional features and functionality, change the appearance of parent theme elements, and add your custom elements. There are different possibilities for this; we will consider the simplest and most understandable ones.

In addition, some of your project's detractors and competitors will not be able to find out what theme you have installed because the child theme will have its proper name.

4.4.2. The Easy Way to Create a Child Theme

Here is the easiest and most reliable way to create a child theme.

Login to *cPanel* and launch *FileManager*. Open the root directory of the site. Open the *wp-content* folder, then the themes folder. You will see here the folder, the name of which will indicate that this folder corresponds to the installed *Neve* theme. Yes, this is where the theme folders are located, and we need to create another folder here (Figure 4-10).

In the */wp-content/themes/* directory, create a directory with the name of the future theme. For example, in our case, let it be called *buildownsite*. After creating the directory, we will open it; it is still empty.

Create a *style.css* file in this directory. Paste this code into it:

```
/**
 * Theme Name: childthemename
 * Template: parentthemename
 */
@import url('../parentthemename/style.css');
```

Replace *"childthemename"* with the name of the theme you are creating. Let it be *"buildownsite"*.

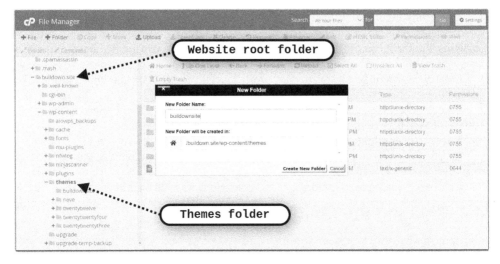

Figure 4-10. cPanel/ File Manager: creating a child theme folder.

Replace *"parentthemename"* with the name of the parent theme. Our theme is *"neve"*. The *style.css* file will look like this:

```
/**
 * Theme Name: buildownsite
 * Template: neve
 */
@import url('../neve/style.css');
```

That's all (Figure 4-11). Save and close the file. We will no longer edit this file. The child theme is created in its minimal configuration. It can already be installed and configured. But first, let's create another file that will be very useful to us.

Figure 4-11. Created *style.css* file.

Create a file *functions.php* (Figure 4-12) in the same directory and insert two lines into it:

```
<?php
// New functions.
```

Figure 4-12. Created *functions.php* file.

We have only added the text of the comment. In this file, we will eventually make small but very practical and useful additions to the functionality of the parent theme.

Save and close the file.

Now, let's check the *Appearance/ Themes* page (Figure 4-13).

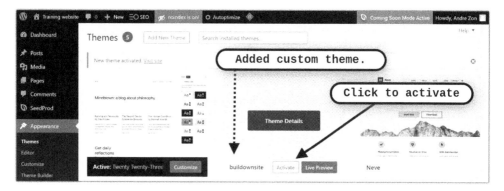

Figure 4-13. Appearance/ Themes page.

The theme we created so quickly and easily right now has appeared on our website and is available for installation. It doesn't have a miniature because we didn't create it. But we see the name, and that's enough.

For now, we are done with creating a child theme and will move on to its installation and configuration.

4.5. Setting Up the Theme

4.5.1. Where to Start Customizing the Theme

The installation and configuration processes of a child and parent theme are no different.

We are working with a child theme.

If you then switch to the parent theme, you will have to configure it separately. If you then return to the child theme, all of its settings will be retained.

This happens because, from the point of view of the *WordPress* system, these are two different themes, and their settings are stored separately.

There is no particular recommended order for setting up a theme. We'll just go through all the settings menu items, and I'll tell you their purpose. We will immediately use some of them to customize the site's appearance.

The theme we chose for training has a pervasive settings menu and a built-in editor of blocks. Using this example, you can learn almost everything useful to you in the future.

So, we simply go through the theme settings menu from top to bottom and perform actions that can be done quickly.

First, we will disable the *Classic Widgets* plugin, which we will not need when setting up this block theme.

We will also disable the *Sassy Social Share* plugin so that it does not take up part of the screen; we will connect and configure it later when preparing the site for opening (Figure 4-14).

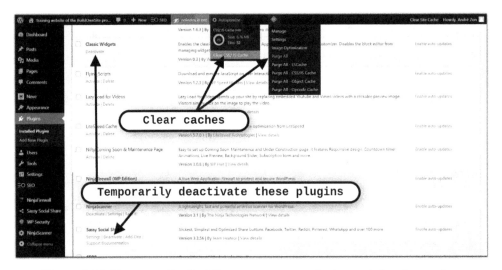

Figure 4-14. Temporarily disabling unnecessary plugins and clearing caches.

Let's clear the cache memory and check the appearance of the main page. There is nothing unnecessary left on it that could interfere with customizing the theme.

4.5.2. Where are Theme Settings?

Now we need to say a few words about the *Appearance* menu (Figure 4-15).

This menu standardly contains *Themes*, *Customize*, *Widgets*, and *Menus* items. This menu may contain additional items added by the theme or plugin.

In our case, there are two additional items - *Theme Builder* and *Options*.

Figure 4-15. The Appearance menu.

The *Options* item refers to the parent theme and contains technical documentation, various useful links to the developer's website, and paid components that expand the theme's capabilities.

We will not use this point now; You can easily deal with these matters on your own when you are ready. You'll be ready for this once you've created a website, populated it with content, and spent some time working with your website in real life.

The *Theme Builder* item, in this case, has nothing to do with the theme. It is added by the "*Coming Soon Page, Maintenance Mode, Landing Pages & WordPress Website Builder by SeedProd*" plugin, the second plugin we tested for hiding a site from visitors. At this point, you can find many options for website design using themes developed by the authors of this plugin. Since we have already selected a theme from another supplier, we will not need this item either.

Just keep in mind that many developers create both themes and plugins. Sometimes, using solutions from one developer can be extremely useful, but this option must be approached carefully and with understanding. Personally, I prefer that the site does not depend on one developer.

Now we need the *Customize* menu item. Behind this item is an extensive submenu that is completely controlled by the installed theme. This means you may see completely different items when you change the theme. There is no need to be afraid of this. After working with the theme we installed, you can easily navigate the customization menu of any other theme.

You can go to customizing the theme through the *Appearance/ Customize* menu item or by clicking the *Customize* button, which is displayed on the themes page over the image of the active theme.

Take a look at the *Appearance/ Customize* menu (Figure 4-16).

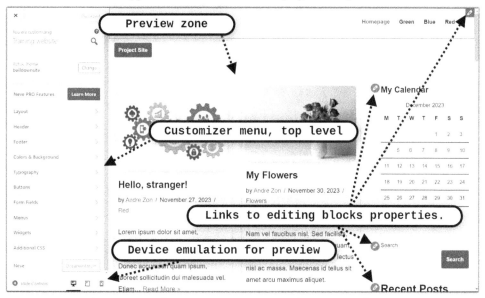

Figure 4-16. The Appearance/ Customize menu and page.

We are not interested in the first and last points related to the capabilities of the extended theme version. Also, we will not use the *Custom CSS* item for now; we will look at it separately.

We are now interested in the items *Layout, Header, Footer, Colors&Background, Typography, Buttons, Form Fields, Menus,* and *Widgets*.

From their names, in general, it is obvious why they are needed, and we will now find out the details. There is quite a lot of information, but it is all quite understandable, and, most importantly, it is perfectly visualized on the right side of the screen.

4.5.3. Setting General Layout Options

Let's start with the *Layout* section (Figure 4-17).

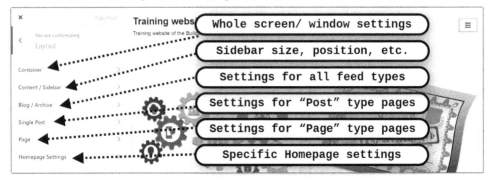

Figure 4-17. Appearance/Customize/Layout menu.

The *Container* item (Figure 4-18) allows you to set the width of the screen area that the content of the site pages will occupy. Please note that here, you can visually evaluate the result for different types of devices - desktop, tablet, and phone.

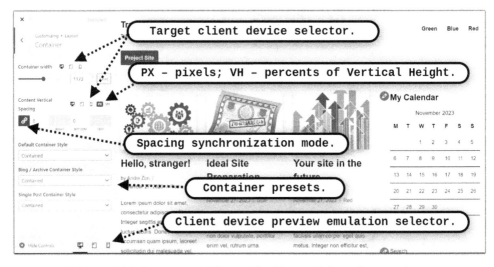

Figure 4-18. Appearance/ Customize/ Layout/ Container settings.

Default Container Style is the default screen settings. They will apply to *Page* posts, search results, and other pages on the site other than the home page, category pages, and individual post pages.

Blog/ Archive Container Style - these are settings for the main page and category pages. *Single Post Container Style* - of course, settings for a single post page.

The container width settings, if the *Contained* type is selected, are the same for all page types.

If you have not successfully changed the container width settings and you need to return to the default values, just click the *Reset* button.

The *Content/ Sidebar* page (Figure 4-19) allows you to configure the presence and placement of a sidebar on site pages. To configure all site pages at once, you need to use the *Sitewide Sidebar Layout* block.

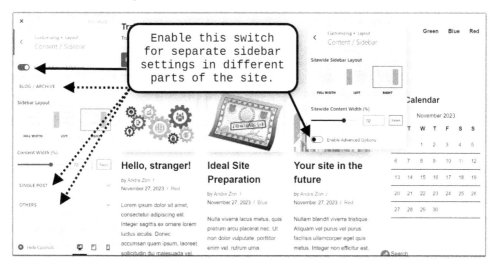

Figure 4-19. Appearance/ Customize/ Layout Content/ Sidebar settings.

To configure sidebar placement for different types of pages, you need to activate the *Enable Advanced Options* switch. In this case, as for setting up a container, you can separately configure the placement of the sidebar for the main page and category pages, the page of an individual post, and all other pages.

Unfortunately, at this point, the developer did not provide a preview on various types of devices.

You can return to the *Layout* item and use this opportunity there. We'll see that for tablets and phones, the sidebar moves to the bottom of the page. This is very convenient and fully corresponds to mobile device users' behavior.

There are no specific recommendations for sidebar width, and the default value of 30 percent seems reasonable.

The *Blog/ Archive* page (Figure 4-20) contains very important settings. With their help, you can quickly and easily change the appearance of the site's main page and site category pages beyond recognition.

Posts can be arranged in a regular linear list or a checkerboard pattern. You can make this list into an impressive matrix of covers or arrange the posts in a grid that is easy to read and clearly shows the illustrations.

The number of columns can be changed from 1 to 4, and the *Masonry* switch gives the page a *Pinterest*-style look with fixed vertical spacing.

The *Enable* featured post section switch allows you to enable the main publication block of the site. The main publication can be either the post published most recently or a post that received a special setting when editing.

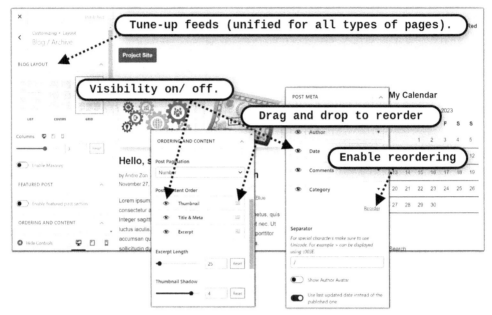

Figure 4-20. Appearance/ Customize/ Layout/ Blog/ Archive settings.

In the *Ordering And Content* block, you can set the desired page turning mode - page number indicators, endless scrolling or page numbers, and a page search field by number. Here, you can configure the display and order of the illustration, title, and metadata, as well as the text passage.

You can specify the length of the passage in the number of words and adjust the shadow cast by the picture.

Please note: if you have activated the *Featured Post* block of the site, then you need to use the infinite scroll mode to scroll through. If you use the page number scrolling mode, then each page will contain the *Featured Post* of the site, and search engines will consider this duplication of content.

When using page numbers, it is best to use as a *Featured Post* some post that does not contain indexable information. This could be, for example, a graphic splash screen or something similar. It is best not to include the *Featured Post* block when using pagination mode.

In the *Post Meta* block, you can configure the composition and appearance of metadata. All of these possibilities are pretty obvious. It's especially interesting to take advantage of the ability to show the date a post was last edited instead of the date it was created. If you regularly update your site, then recent dates will make a very favorable impression on site visitors.

The *Single Post* page (Figure 4-21) contains a lot of settings that control the appearance of the individual post page. The top part of the post can be configured separately. Please note: in *Cover* mode, the sidebar in the desktop layout moves down below the illustration. In this mode, you can customize the placement of text and illustrations in a variety of ways.

In the main part of the post, you can control the display and order of content, a list of tags, a form for submitting comments, and navigation links that allow you to go to the previous and next posts.

The form for sending comments is also customizable separately. You can customize the padding, colors, styles, and labels for the header and button.

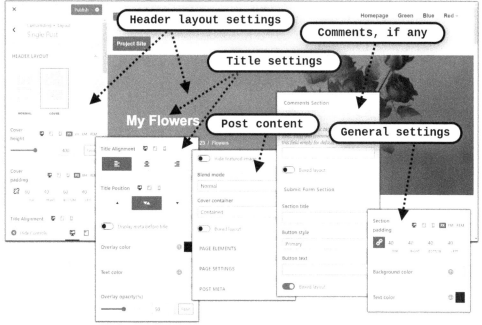

Figure 4-21. Appearance/ Customize/ Layout/ Single Post settings.

There is little customization on a *Page* because a *Page* is a stand-alone publication type that is specifically designed to have its own original design, its own content, and its own functionality. Even linking pages to categories and tags is not provided. Therefore, only such settings are provided for pages that ensure stylistic unity of the pages with the rest of the site (Figure 4-22).

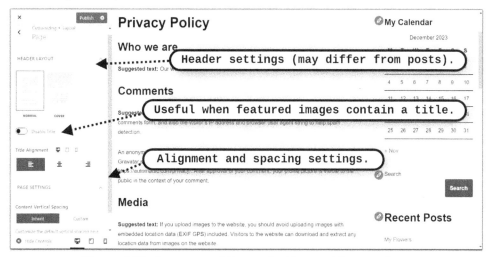

Figure 4-22. Appearance/ Customize/ Layout/ Page settings.

You can choose how to place the illustration, align the title horizontally, or remove it completely.

Of course, the header and footer settings for the pages are saved, which are the same for the entire site. We will also talk about them now.

The last item in the *Layout* section is *Homepage Settings*. This item simply duplicates the capabilities of the *Settings/ Reading* page, which we talked about when we set up *WordPress* on the site.

We've gone through the entire *Layout* section. As you have seen, it has a lot of settings, which together give a very large number of possible options for the appearance of the site pages. This type of settings system is typical for popular top themes.

But this is not all. Such noticeable and important parts of pages as the header and footer are customized using their own tools. At the same time, block technology shows all its specifics and all its capabilities.

4.5.4. Header and Footer Customization

A header is not just some kind of area for placing elements. This is a rather complex structure.

Let's study this structure. The header part structure for our theme is quite typical (Figure 4-23). It consists of three horizontal stripes: the top of the header, the main part, and the bottom part.

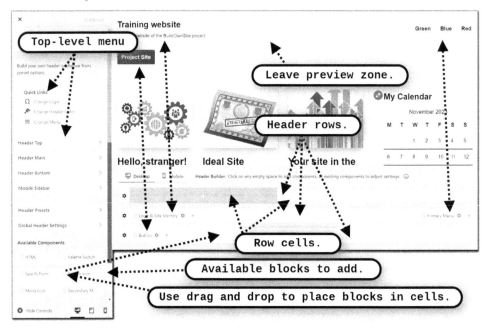

Figure 4-23. Appearance/Customize/Header settings.

Block technology is used to edit their content (Figure 4-24). Blocks can be moved and configured individually. Try moving the existing blocks to the top and then putting them back in place. As you can see, it's very simple. If you click on the settings icon on a block, the settings for that particular block will appear on the sidebar.

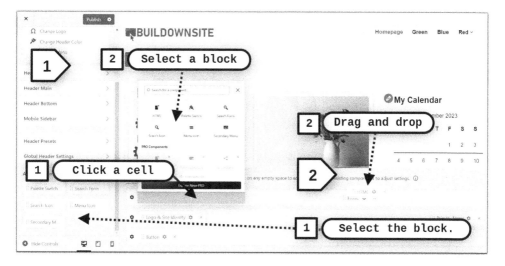

Figure 4-24. Appearance/ Customize/ Header/ Row: adding blocks.

We will return to the *Logo & Site Identity* block at the stage of preparing the site for opening and consider in detail all its capabilities.

The *Primary Menu* block currently consists of one link, which was added by the WordPress installer just for example. We will configure the composition of the menu separately, but now we'll just take a closer look at its settings on the left sidebar .

The settings (Figure 4-25) are grouped into 3 tabs: *General*, *Layout*, and *Style*. These tabs have a fairly obvious purpose and typical sets of tools for each of them.

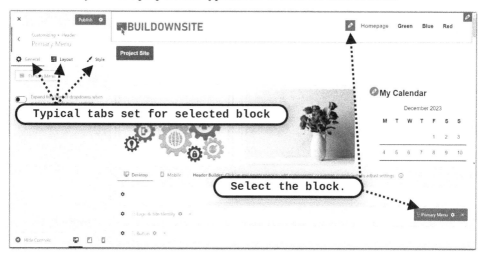

Figure 4-25. Appearance/ Customize/ Header/ Primary Menu/ Settings.

The *General* tab (Figure 4-26) contains a link to edit the menu itself and a switch that activates drop-down menus on mobile devices. If you do not activate it, the menu will be displayed as a linear list, which will contain all nested items. This option is the best for mobile devices, so it is used by default.

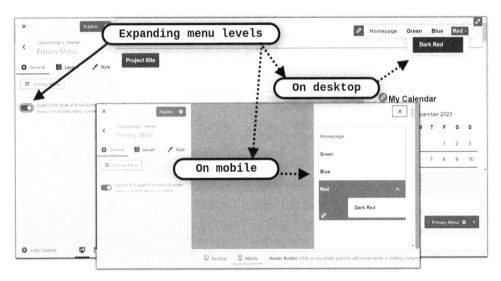

Figure 4-26. Appearance/ Customize/ Header/ Primary Menu/ Settings/ General.

On the *Layout* tab (Figure 4-27), you can configure the dimensions, margins, and padding for the rectangles corresponding to menu items.

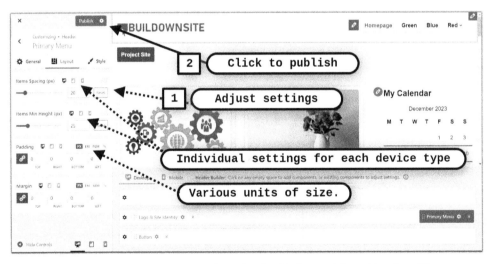

Figure 4-27. Appearance/ Customize/ Header/ Primary Menu/ Settings/ Layout.

On the *Style* tab (Figure 4-28), you can select a skin, colors, and font, as well as adjust text parameters.

If we return to the header settings section, we will see that, using the menu, you can configure each of its horizontal stripes separately.

Each of these zones has its own *Layout* and *Style* tabs, similar to those we just saw for the *Primary Menu* block   (Figure 4-29); with these tools, you can configure common content display settings for each header zone.

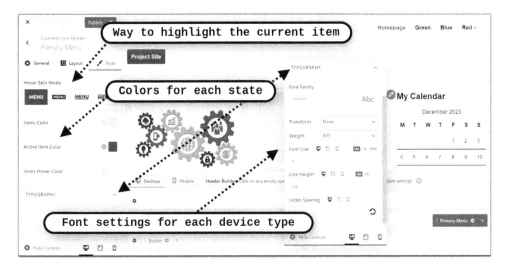

Figure 4-28. Appearance/ Customize/ Header/ Primary Menu/ Settings/ Style.

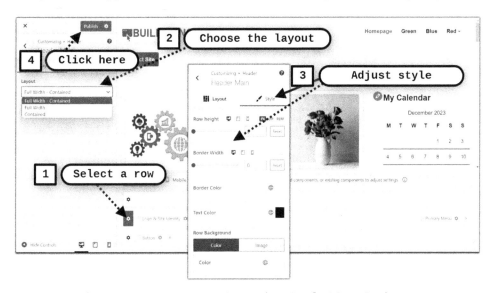

Figure 4-29. Appearance/ Customize/ Header/ Row Settings.

This combination of block technology and classic tools gives a lot of freedom and flexibility when customizing the look. There is one item left in the header settings block that we haven't said anything about yet. It's called *Mobile Sidebar* (Figure 4-30). What does it have to do with the header? The most direct.

The fact is that on mobile devices, the classic header, consisting of wide horizontal stripes and horizontal elements located inside these stripes, simply cannot be displayed without loss of readability. Therefore, on the screen of a tablet and phone, it is automatically transformed into a vertically oriented structure. This is very convenient, meets the natural expectations of the user, and characterizes the theme as "responsive."

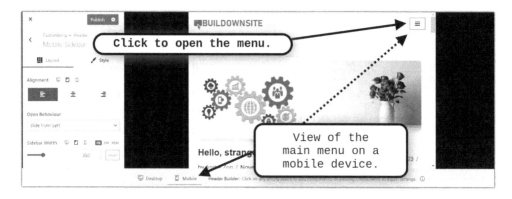

Figure 4-30. Appearance/ Customize/ Header/ Mobile Sidebar menu.

Here, on the *Layout* tab (Figure 4-31), you can set the width of the mobile sidebar panel, content alignment, and how it appears on the screen.

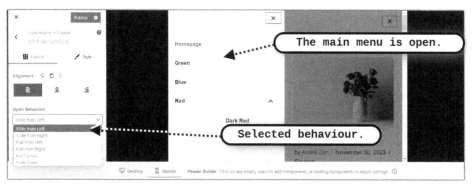

Figure 4-31. Appearance/ Customize/ Header/ Mobile Sidebar/ Layout menu.

On the *Style* tab (Figure 4-32), you can customize the text and background colors and even select a background image.

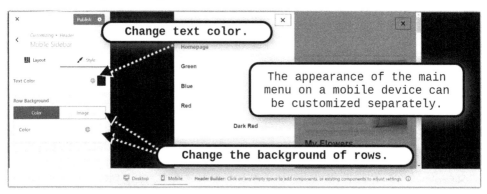

Figure 4-32. Appearance/ Customize/ Header/ Mobile Sidebar/ Style menu.

We won't change many settings for now but will simply add a button to the bottom of the header with a link to the project's information site. It's very simple (Figure 4-33). You need to click on the "+" icon, select a button from the list of components, and add the link *https://buildownsite.com* and the inscription "*Project Site*" to it. It turned out to be a very useful button.

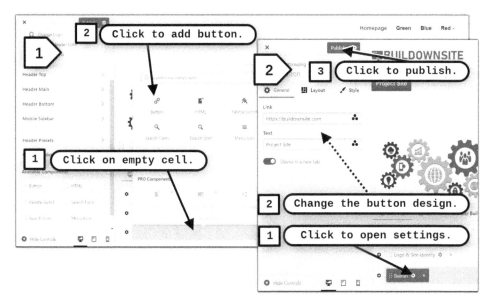

Figure 4-33. Appearance/Customize/Header/add button menu.

At the bottom of the header settings menu, there is a *Header Presets* item. Here, you can quickly select the most suitable layout option, the settings of which can then be refined (Figure 4-34).

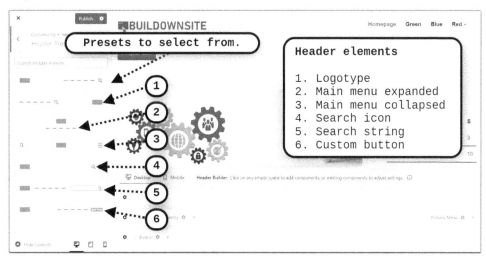

Figure 4-34. Appearance/ Customize/ Header/ Header Presets menu.

The *Global Header Settings* item allows you to define the general background for the header.

At the very bottom of the sidebar, there is a list of available components.

For free version of the theme, it is small, but it does have a universal component: "*HTML Block.*"

You don't need to be a technical expert to use it, just basic knowledge that is easy to find. We will check this in practice when preparing the site for opening after filling it with content.

In this section of the settings, we just need to figure out why pencil icons are needed in various parts of the header. It's very simple: *Shift+Click* on these icons to activate the settings menu for the element, which is automatically framed under the mouse cursor (Figure 4-35).

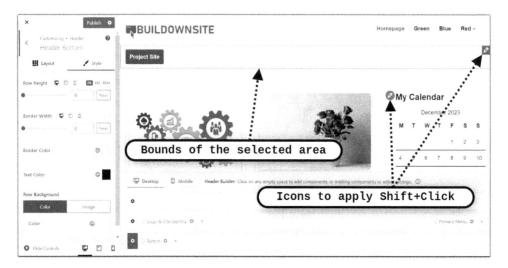

Figure 4-35. Activating settings using Shift-Click.

This is another very simple and convenient way to access the features that we have already explored.

When you click on these icons, the corresponding menu is displayed in the left sidebar, and the element settings icon is highlighted at the bottom of the screen on the block control panel.

Let's go back to the main A*ppearance/Customize* menu. Here, we have a few more points awaiting us, which now, based on existing knowledge, will not be difficult to understand.

The footer block in our theme, similar to the header, consists of three horizontal stripes. They are also divided into cells, but their number can be set in the range from 1 to 5.

In addition to the layout, you can customize style elements for each horizontal footer zone.

To set the contents of the footer, you must first place special elements from the block called *Available Components* in the right places in the template (Figure 4-36). Only then inside these elements, it will be possible to place the necessary information.

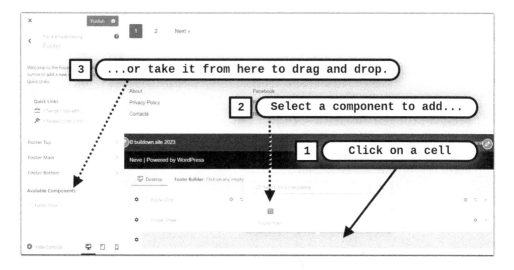

Figure 4-36. Appearance/ Customize/ Footer/ Available Components menu.

This two-step system exists to ensure compatibility with traditional technology, which we will look at when learning how to work with the classic theme.

In the case of a classic theme, everything is more uncomplicated, but when working with a block theme, you just need to know this feature. Maybe in the future, developers will simplify this technique.

Let's place the *Footer One* module in the footer cell for clarity (Figure 4-37). We can configure the general parameters for placing information, and insert a block of the type we need into the module, and then configure this block. There are corresponding icons on the module for this purpose.

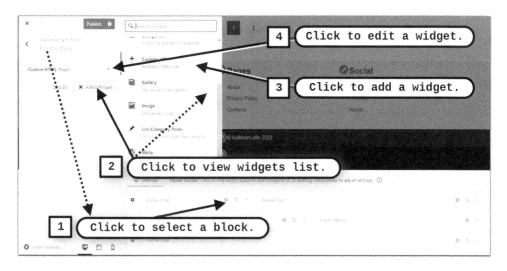

Figure 4-37. Appearance/ Customize/ Footer/ Footer One menu.

This is the now traditional way of customizing the appearance using block technology. Some may find it too complicated and long. Well, block technology is just beginning its journey, and more effective solutions will certainly be found in the future. As you remember, I promised to show you an alternative way - using the classic theme.

In the meantime, we continue to get acquainted with the theme settings.

4.5.5. Customizing Colors and Fonts

The next item is *Colors & Background* (Figure 4-38). Everything here is very simple, but it is impressive. Here, you can create palettes for the entire site and select the one you need from among them. The theme "out of the box" comes in two ready-made palettes - light and dark. And if you wish, you can create and use your own palette!

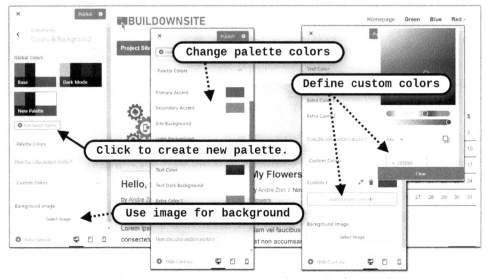

Figure 4-38. Appearance/ Customize/ Colors & Background menu.

The *Typography* item (Figure 4-39) is responsible for setting fonts - global for the entire site, for headings, and for texts. Nothing is unexpected here - you can select a font and adjust its size, thickness, line height, and spacing between characters.

Please note: On the *Typography/ General* page, there is an option to enable the *Fallback Font (Local Fonts Hosting)* feature. The fact is that the theme uses *Google Fonts*, which are loaded in real-time. If something goes wrong and, for some reason, these fonts cannot be loaded, then this setting can be very useful.

Using *Google Fonts* and generally loading fonts in real-time is now standard practice. However, it is believed that this is not very good for the site's speed, and some experts advise using fonts installed directly on the server. This is possible - you just need to activate the *Local* fonts hosting switch on the *Typography* page.

Do not do that, at least at the initial stage of the site's operation.

Google Fonts is more than just a repository of about 1,000 free fonts. This is a fairly smart and fast system that works very efficiently and is constantly being improved. When you're done setting up your site, at the advanced optimization stage, you'll simply check whether switching to local font storage gives a noticeable improvement in site speed or not. For now, this question is best left for the future.

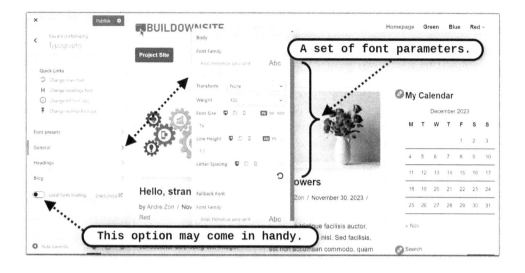

Figure 4-39. Appearance/ Customize/ Typography/ General menu.

Pay attention to the settings on the *Typography/Headings* page (Figure 4-40). Here, you will see the designations *H1...H6*, each of which corresponds to a separate settings block containing parameters already familiar to us. These are font size and weight, font transformation, line height, and character spacing. What is this all for?

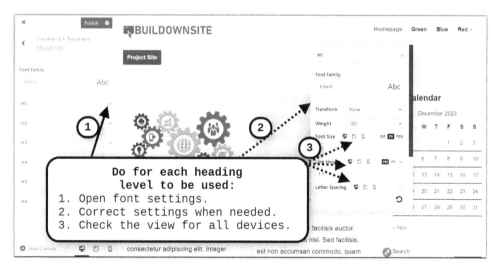

Figure 4-40. Appearance/ Customize/ Typography/ Headings menu.

It's simple: *H1...H6* are designations for heading levels that are used in publications on the site. Check whether these headings are easy to read and whether their settings need to be changed, at least for levels *H1*, *H2*, and *H3*. Now I will explain to you what is the matter.

Headings on site pages have a hierarchy. Every page should have an *H1* heading. This is a page-level heading. If there are several publications or posts on a page, then one of them can be the main one and have a page-level heading (if such a heading is not on the page itself), that is, *H1*. If there is no main publication on the page, then within the page code, this heading level should correspond to the title of this page.

If you create a post, its title will automatically turn into an *H1* title when published.

It is recommended to divide the text inside the post into parts, each of which has an *H2* level heading. Within each of these parts, there should be parts with *H3* level headings and so on. There can be a total of 6 levels of headings. The level with the lower number must always be higher than the level with the higher number. You cannot skip levels.

Visually, when a post is displayed on a website page, the user should see the difference in the font of the headings. The *H1* level should have the largest font size, the *H2* level should have a smaller font size, the *H3* level should have an even smaller font size, etc.

This practice comes from traditional printing, so the user expects it will not be violated.

Our task is to adjust the headings' font so that the user's expectations are not deceived and that the headings are sized to match the size of the device screen. Therefore, it is very important to set the size of headings so that they are easy to read and look aesthetically pleasing.

One thing to remember is that the use of *H1, H2,* and *H3* headings is especially useful for *SEO* and is checked by both search engine bots and *SEO* plugins. Of course, as long as these headings are used correctly and contain keywords. We'll return to this issue when we explore text content creation. For now, just keep in mind that *H1, H2,* and *H3* headings should be used extensively in publications whenever possible. Therefore, their appearance is essential. There is one more rule that we will implement in the next step. It concerns the colors used for headings and body text.

On the *Typography/Blog* page (Figure 4-41), as you might guess, fonts are configured for all elements of publications. Why is this page called this? Probably just for brevity's sake. If you have a "*Blog*" category on your website, then you don't need to think that these are the settings specifically for it. These are settings common to all post types.

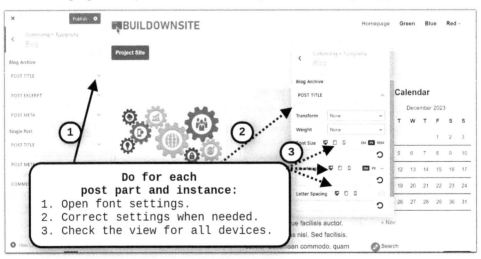

Figure 4-41. Appearance/ Customize/ Typography/ Blog menu.

There are two settings blocks here.

The *Blog Archive* block is all the pages of the site on which posts are displayed in a brief form.

These include the home page, category pages, search results pages, and post pages for specific tags. Here you can customize fonts for titles, excerpts, and metadata.

The *Single Post* block is, as you already understood, pages corresponding to individual posts on the site, as well as independent pages. Here you can customize fonts for titles, metadata, and comment replies. The font for the main text, as you remember, is configured on the *Typography/ General* page, which we already talked about.

Next page - *Buttons* (Figure 4-42). Here you can configure the general properties of labels for buttons, as well as define two appearance styles for buttons - *Primary* and *Secondary*.

There are settings for the overall style - filled or border, font colors, background or border colors, corner radii, and button shadow. When you add buttons to your content, you can choose which of these styles should be used.

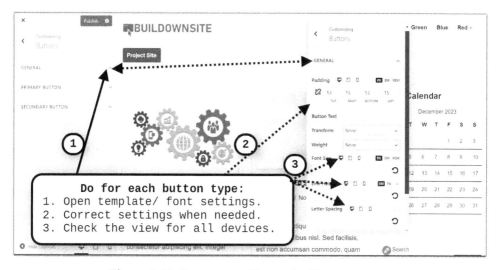

Figure 4-42. Appearance/Customize/Buttons menu.

Note the customization of the button's appearance when the mouse pointer is over it. This setting is also set separately for each of the two styles.

On the *Form Fields* page (Figure 4-43), using the same technology, you can configure the general properties of form fields, fonts for text input fields, and labels for these fields, and also select the style of the buttons.

This refers to the choice between the *Primary* and *Secondary* styles, which we just talked about in relation to buttons.

We have fully reviewed the capabilities of the *Customize* settings block for our theme. This, as I promised, is quite a large amount of information, but it is important to be able to navigate it.

Since you will be accessing this settings block quite often, you will soon get used to it. This block may differ for other themes, but you will easily learn to navigate them when the need arises.

There are two items left in this block - *Menus* and *Widgets*.

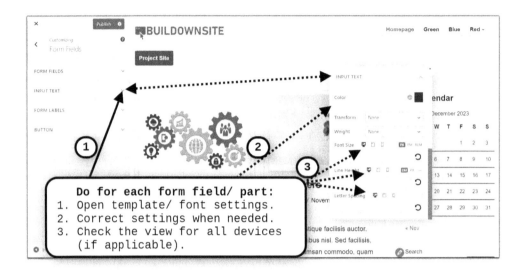

Figure 4-43. Appearance/Customize/Form Fields menu.

4.5.6. More About Theme Settings

We will study the *Menus* item in detail when we set up the site's main menu.

The capabilities of the *Widgets* block are mainly limited to the sidebar. We are not considering *Shop Sidebar* because we are creating an informational site. Setting it up is no different from setting up the *Sidebar* block.

The principle, as usual, is very simple: you need to add blocks from the available ones to the sidebar and drag them to the desired position. Each widget can be further customized separately.

Working with classic theme widgets looks similar, but they have their own features and capabilities. We'll talk about this a little later.

We've now looked at customizing the look and feel of a typical high-quality modern block theme. You can see that there are a lot of blocks; they are varied and form a flexible and powerful system that allows you to manage the appearance of your site easily and effectively.

However, such a system also has its limitations.

Part of these limitations is that it is simply impossible to create an absolutely universal system that could provide for any need.

The only way to master such capabilities is to become a universal and omnipotent web programmer, but that is not what we are talking about.

Another part of these restrictions is due to the fact that developers of universal themes offer to remove restrictions through the use of specialized site templates and various extensions. Of course, this justifiably costs money, and, sooner or later, many website owners purchase themes that they are completely satisfied with.

Beginner developers and inexperienced website owners should not rush into purchases. You need to study the *WordPress* system and accurately formulate your website's requirements. This takes time, experience and knowledge. We are still beginning our journey, and our needs are quite modest.

Some of these needs are very important in practice. I mean the need to unify design elements in accordance with your requirements for the style of the site. For example, you may need to add links to external sites to your text and give those links a look and feel the theme does not intend that. Or round the corners of elements when the theme does not provide for this.

Such opportunities are provided by the technology provided by the *WordPress* system for creating a custom *CSS* file that is associated with the active theme and complements it.

So that you know what we're talking about, *CSS* stands for *Cascading Style Sheets*. This is a special declarative language that can be used to describe the appearance and simple behavior of website page elements. This is one of the traditional technologies that professional website developers own.

We will limit ourselves to fairly simple and practical recipes for a few cases. This is necessary so that you understand how to use this opportunity.

4.6. Customizing the Theme with CSS File

4.6.1. CSS Capabilities for a WordPress Site

A custom *CSS* file is a very powerful and convenient way to customize the appearance of a website to your liking and in accordance with your goals and needs.

This method can be used to work with any theme, both parent and child.

Of course, to fully work with such a file, you need to have knowledge of the *CSS* language.

Now you won't need such knowledge: I will give you several ready-made simple examples that you can use and to which it will be easy for you to make changes. In the future, based on this information, you can make a decision about how you will use this technology.

The *CSS* language is not complex, and there is a lot of documentation on it. If necessary, you will be able to use those features that you need. You most likely will not have to study it completely since this is not necessary.

Very often, simple tricks are implemented using *CSS* - hiding unnecessary template elements, changing the color and size of inscriptions and headings, rounding the corners of rectangles and images, etc.

We said above that there is a specific rule regarding using colors for headings.

This rule generally states that the smaller the font size, the more the text color should contrast with the background color.

For example, if the body text is black and the *H1* headings should be bright red for site design reasons, then the heading font should get smaller and darker as the level number increases, reaching black or almost black at *H6*.

This rule is due to two reasons.

The first is quite obvious: it is difficult for the user to read small letters if they do not have enough contrast in relation to the background.

The second reason is that if the search engine bot finds that the text is not readable enough because it is small or has insufficient color contrast, it will lower your site's Core Web Vitals scores, which is bad. Therefore, font colors, as well as their sizes, matter.

Unfortunately, not all themes allow you to do this easily and exactly as you need. This is one of the situations where it is impossible to do without creating your own *CSS* file.

Here's how it's done.

4.6.2. CSS Usage Examples

4.6.2.1. Hiding Page Elements

The first example is hiding unnecessary elements. This technique is often used when the theme does not provide such an option.

It may be advisable to hide elements of page templates that do not meet the requirements for the appearance of pages, that is, unnecessary elements. Sometimes, this method is used in the interests of site security.

It happens when site owners need to hide the names of plugins, themes, and even the fact that the site is built on *WordPress*. We will still consider security issues when solving problems of website maintenance and support, and we will definitely study this issue in more detail.

For now, let's take the obvious first step (Figure 4-44): start by hiding visible information. Let's hide the line in the footer that contains the theme name.

To do this, we first need to determine the *ID* of the element we want to hide or the name of its class:

- right-click on the target element,
- select *Inspect* from the context menu,
- on the right side of the window, find the target element and its container,
- copy the name of the container or its class (in our case it is *component-wrap*),
- prepare the necessary code in *CSS*,
- paste this code into the window on the *Customize/Additional CSS* page,
- click the *Publish* button,
- open the site page and clear the cache if necessary.

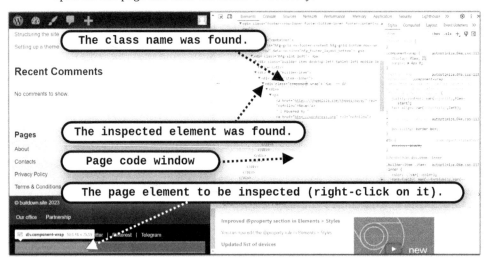

Figure 4-44. Inspecting screenshot to find and copy a class name.

We are using this simple code:

```
.component-wrap {
    display:none;
}
```

Please note that the class name in this code must begin with a dot.

Ready. The element is hidden. Now, in its place, we can display, for example, a copyright notice. We will do this when preparing the site for opening.

Add the code, click the "*Publish*" button, open the page, and clear the cache.

Attention: remember that this method of hiding elements in this case is not the best solution since the search engine robot will detect actual hyperlinks that exist but are not displayed on the page (Figure 4-45). Actually, this method is very well known, and some experts recommend using it; I don't consider it possible for me to join them.

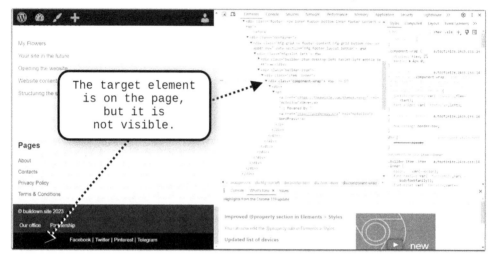

Figure 4-45. The page with a hidden element.

Perhaps it would be better to buy a paid professional version of the theme, which provides not only for hiding unnecessary blocks with links but also for freely manipulating such blocks.

4.6.2.2. Changing the Appearance of Page Elements

The following example is changing the appearance of existing elements.

The relevant element is the page numbers and buttons in the pagination block. We'll make the font a little larger, round the corners, and change the color of the active buttons.

First, let's define the class names for these elements.

In this case, these are *page-numbers* for the entire block and *page-numbers.current* for the current page number, which has a different background color and a different font type.

This is our code.

```
.page-numbers.current {
    text-align:center;
    font-size: 1.2rem !important;
    font-weight: 600;
    color: #000000 !important;
    background-color: #cccccc !important;
    text-decoration: none;
height: 32px;
    padding: 8px 16px 18px 16px;
    border-radius: 16px 16px 16px 16px;
}
```

```
a.page-numbers {
    text-align:center;
    font-size: 1.1rem !important;
    font-weight: 600;
    color: #ffffff !important;
    background-color: #cc0033 !important;
    text-decoration: none;
height: 32px;
    padding: 8px 16px 18px 16px;
border-radius: 16px 16px 16px 16px;
}

a.page-numbers:link {
    text-decoration: none;
    padding: 8px 16px 18px 16px;
    border-radius: 16px 16px 16px 16px;
}

a.page-numbers:active {
    padding: 8px 16px 18px 16px;
    text-decoration: none;
    border-radius: 16px 16px 16px 16px;
}

a.page-numbers:hover {
    padding: 8px 16px 18px 16px;
    color: #ffffff !important;
    background-color: #337ab7 !important;
    box-shadow: 0px 0px 24px rgba(153,153,255,1.0);
    border-radius: 16px 16px 16px 16px;
}
```

Please note that the names of element classes that must contain a hyperlink are preceded by the letter "*a.*" This should always be done if the style of an element containing a hyperlink is modified.

Add the code, click the "*Publish*" button, open the page, and clear the cache.

Ready. We not only changed the appearance of the block and its elements but also made it more interactive - when you hover the mouse, the elements change their appearance. For this, we used the "*hover*" modifier. Remember we already met it when customizing the theme?

4.6.2.3. Changing the Appearance of Various Blocks

The third example is changing the settings of a block containing images and posts on blog pages. If your site contains non-technical information, but, for example, lifestyle information, then rounded corners will be very useful.

Let's start with the images. This requires very simple code.

```
.wp-post-image {
    border-radius: 1.2rem 1.2rem 1.2rem 1.2rem;
}
```

To visually separate posts from each other, we'll round the corners of the post announcements and add shadows that grow larger when hovering the mouse.

Here's the code that does it.

```
.article-content-col {
    padding: 10px 12px 12px 12px;
    background-color: #ffffff !important;
    border-radius: 1.8rem 1.8rem 1.8rem 1.8rem;
    font-size: 1.2rem;
    color: #000000 !important;
    font-weight: 400;
    box-shadow: 0px 0px 6px rgba(153,153,153,0.6);
}

.article-content-col:hover {
    box-shadow: 0px 0px 24px rgba(153,153,255,0.8);
}
```

Look at the post page. We can change the appearance of any of its elements.

For example, let it be a title format. Let's make it similar to the other modified elements - reduce the font, change its color, and make a rectangle with rounded short sides as the background.

```
.title.entry-title {
    padding: 10px 16px 12px 16px;
    background-color: rgba(204,204,204,0.8);
    border-radius: 1.8rem 1.8rem 1.8rem 1.8rem;
    font-size: 1.4rem;
    color: #000000 !important;
    font-weight: 600;
    box-shadow: 0px 0px 6px rgba(153,153,153,0.6);
}
```

Add the code, click the "*Publish*" button, open the page, and clear the cache.

4.6.2.4. Links in the Form of Buttons

And one more example. Let's add our own element and customize its appearance. This will be a regular link that will look like a flat button with rounded short sides. We will call the class for it "*simplink*". Here is a code snippet for this class.

```
.simplink {
    color: #cc0033;
    background-color: #ffffff;
    text-align: center;
    line-height: 2.6rem;
    padding: 8px 16px 8px 16px;
    border-radius: 1.2rem 1.2rem 1.2rem 1.2rem;
    border-width: 2px !important;
        border-style: solid !important;
        border-color: #cc0033 !important;
    white-space: pre;
}

A.simplink:hover {
    color: #ffffff !important;
    background-color: #cc0033;
    border-color: #cc0033 !important;
}
```

Publish your modified CSS file.

Now, you need to add two links to the text of the post on the site. We will leave one of them in its standard form and bind the class we created to the other. This is easiest in the Classic Editor, in "Text" mode.

You need to insert this simple HTML code into the text of the post:

```
<p><a href="https://buildown.site">Homepage</a></p>
<p><a class="simplink" href="https://buildown.site">Homepage</a></p>
```

Publish the modified post. Open the post page and clear the cache. Now you can see the difference.

We've looked at a few simple tricks that will help you personalize your site's pages, no matter what theme you're using. Of course, this is just the beginning, and the capabilities of this technology require a deeper dive into the *CSS* language.

If you need it, now you know what to do. If simple, ready-made solutions are enough for you, then now you have them, and you can experiment with them by changing the parameter values.

Tip for the future: To make it easier to recover everything you wrote in this file if necessary, always keep a copy of its contents on your computer as a simple text (*.txt*) file. To do this, you need to select the *CSS* code in the left sidebar, copy it to the clipboard, and then paste it into a regular text file using a regular text editor. The file can be saved with the usual *.txt* extension; this does not affect anything in the *CSS* code.

We did not discuss or comment on the purpose and syntax of code elements here. They are fairly self-explanatory, and the best way to learn how to use them is in the *CSS* reference material.

Here, we simply do not have the opportunity to study them; they are too voluminous, deserve a separate, very long, and detailed consideration, and require basic technical training. If you are interested in the specifics of working with *CSS*, then your best bet is to find a handy reference book so that you have precise tips at hand for all cases.

4.7. Classic Theme Usage

4.7.1. Installing the Classic Theme

To give you a better understanding of how to work with *WordPress* themes, we will temporarily install another theme that does not use block technology at all.

Why is this necessary? Of course, only a competent developer or site owner can consciously choose between a difficult-to-customize modern block theme and a classic one. Only he can decide which theme he needs.

Now that we've looked at the basic free version of a modern, high-quality block theme in some detail, it's easier to articulate why you might need a classic theme.

There are thousands of classic themes in the official repository on *https://wordpress.org* and thousands on third-party commercial sites. They are regularly improved and updated, and there are more and more of them because there is a demand for them that is not decreasing.

The thing is that classic themes are usually easier to customize, they are ready to work out of the box, they work faster, and - most importantly - they have specialization.

This means that among them, you can find a theme that is as close as possible to the desired result and customize it very quickly and easily. Look at what classic themes are available in the official *WordPress* website repository: one of them may be the one you need.

We will check out the *Twenty Twelve* theme (Figure 4-46) from the *WordPress* developers. This is a typical classic theme; it was created back in 2012! This theme is updated regularly: at the time of writing this book, the last update was made in November 2023. The theme is responsive and balanced; it has very good feedback statistics and remains relevant. Therefore, it can be useful not only for training but also for creating a simple informational website or blog.

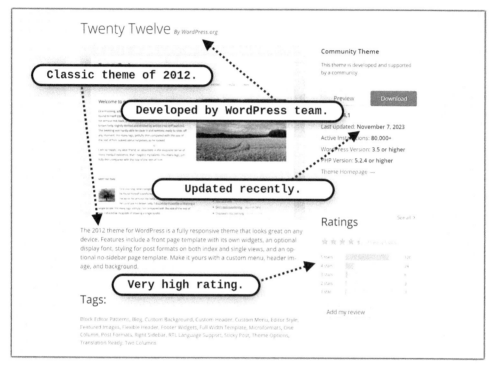

Figure 4-46. The classic theme page on the official website.

We will install and activate this theme, as well as the *Classic Widgets* plugin since we will need it to customize the appearance of the pages.

4.7.2. Customizing the Classic Theme

As with all other themes, the main settings for the appearance of the site are on the *Appearance/ Customize* page (Figure 4-47).

The settings are elementary: you can adjust the color of the header text, the background text of the page in the browser window, add an image to the header, add a background image to the page and configure its display, configure the main menu, and set the desired location of widgets.

As you can see, everything is very simple, especially after everything we have seen for a complex block theme. Of course, we are looking at a very simple theme. It inherited not only simple customization principles but also traditional approaches to website design. There are a huge number of much more complex classical themes.

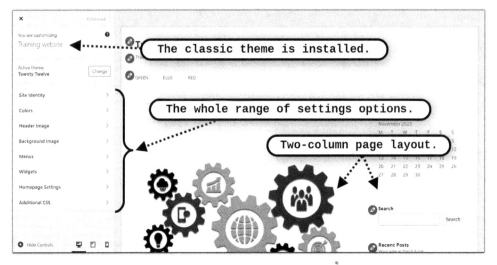

Figure 4-47. Appearance/Customize: general settings.

The main thing in this case is not the complexity of the theme or the number of its settings. Did you notice that we still haven't said anything about widgets?

Instead of the *Appearance/ Customize/ Widgets* page (Figure 4-48), open the *Appearance/ Widgets* page. You see something completely new, which is actually a forgotten old thing. More precisely - classic.

On the left side of the screen, there are many rectangles with various inscriptions, and above them, there is a heading *Available Widgets*.

Each such rectangle represents a widget. The widget collection consists of standard *WordPress* widgets that have always existed and widgets that can add themes and plugins.

On the right side of the screen, large rectangles show areas of the pages in which widgets can be placed.

Currently, in the *Main Sidebar* area, there are three widgets called *Block*. This name makes no sense, and inside the widgets, we see some codes.

These are just traces left in the system by the block theme that we have already configured.

For now, we can simply ignore them or drag them to the Inactive *Widgets* area, which is located in the lower left part of the screen - they will be useful to us when we finish working with the classic theme and return to the block theme.

Now, let's look at the main page of the site.

The right sidebar is empty. We can return widgets that were already there, or add others from those available. Let's add a C*alendar* widget and a *Categories* widget. If we don't need some widget, for example, *Categories*, then we can simply return it back to the zone of available widgets; we can do that, too.

Instead, we will place the *Recent Posts* widget in the right sidebar. Let's go to the main page of the site and clear the cache. The widgets we added appeared in the right sidebar.

Let's return to the widget management page.

Widgets have very simple settings, and it is impossible to get confused with them. This is very good for novice website creators and, in general, for people who are far from technology.

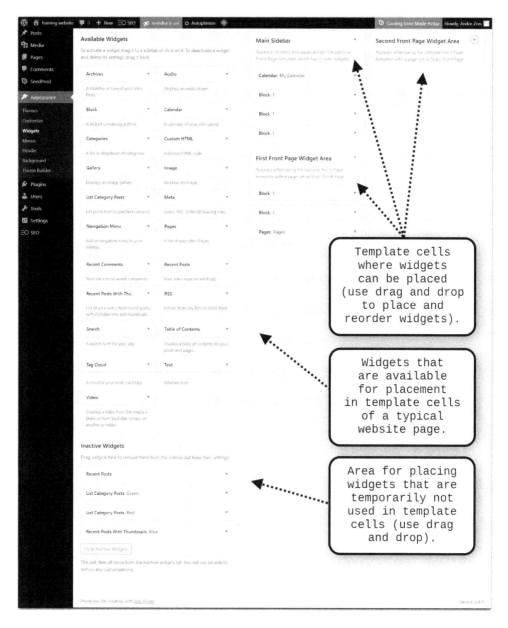

Figure 4-48. Appearance/Widget options.

4.7.3. Additional Widget Capabilities

Ease of customization isn't the only benefit of classic themes and classic widgets.

The fact is that this technology has existed for a long time, and many plugins have been created for it, which significantly expand the capabilities of the widget system. It could be argued that many of these features are still unavailable to next-generation block themes.

151

To make sure of this, we will install and activate the *Widget Options* plugin. Now, we'll see what's changed on the *Appearance/Widgets* page (Figure 4-49).

The number of widget settings has increased, and among them, there is something very interesting.

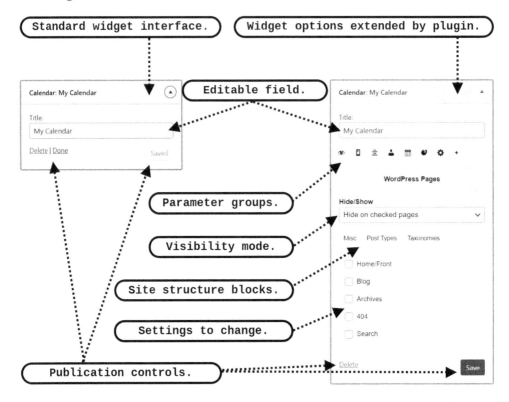

Figure 4-49. Widget settings using the Widget Options plugin, an example.

Take a closer look at these new settings: for each widget, you can set its display mode!

Now, any widget can be shown or, conversely, hidden in specified categories, on specified pages, on tag pages, and on standard website pages. You can also provide for displaying or hiding widgets on mobile devices. And all this is customizable for each widget individually!

You probably already understand what opportunities this provides. Widgets and related posts can be displayed on the same page. This is very useful for affiliate sales, for example.

There are other handy solutions that were originally developed for classic themes. These are different options for lists of posts instead of theme templates for the main page and category pages. These are filter systems that will make it easier for the user to find a publication or product on your website. These are various additional navigation elements, social widgets, and much more.

Many of these solutions are compatible with block themes, but for classic themes, there is a much larger choice.

Now you know the main differences between classic themes. This is thematic specialization, ease of configuration, and the presence of a huge number of additional solutions that simply and effectively perform complex tasks.

The choice of the type of theme and the theme itself is, of course, yours. You now know how to customize different types of themes and understand their differences and capabilities.

Let's return to our main block theme (we use Neve) and start checking the appearance of the site.

4.8. Checking Website Look

4.8.1. Why is an Intermediate Check Needed and Where to Start?

This is a very simple and short job, but it is incredibly important. Here we check the appearance of the site we created.

The purpose of the audit is to determine what needs additional or re-tuning, what was missed, and what needs to be done from scratch.

We're building a relatively simple informational site, but it contains everything you need to get started as a professional, and we've fully explored customizing it using a modern, high-quality block theme.

When checking the appearance of the site after changing the theme settings, you need to follow a simple rule: completely clear the *LiteSpeed* plugin cache and the *Autoptimize* plugin cache.

These plugins cache not only all the principal codes of the site's pages but also, in particular, information from the very style sheets that are stored in *CSS* files and are responsible for designing the appearance of the site. You already know all this.

If you do not clear the cache after changing the site's appearance settings, the site's pages may look the same as if no settings were made.

Therefore, never forget about the plugin cache.

Additionally, your browser may store old stylesheets in its own cache.

Depending on the browser version and settings, this may also affect the appearance of the site. Therefore, it is very useful to consult your browser's documentation to know how to clear its cache if necessary.

So, to check the appearance of the site, we clear the plugin cache.

Then we simply visually check how the elements that we configured look on the site pages.

You may have a question: why bother additionally checking the appearance of the site if we have already seen everything when we configured the theme in the *Appearance* menu?

Never try to check the appearance of the site on the theme settings pages in the *Appearance* menu!

The thing is that the theme settings preview window:
- always contains elements needed for configuration but not used on the site,
- has a smaller width than the actual browser window,
- does not always show page elements in their real form, which should correspond to the settings.

The reasons are quite significant, and they always exist. Therefore, you should always check real pages and not their appearance in the interface of configuration tools.

4.8.2. Visual Check Sequence

Here is an approximate procedure for visual inspection.

1. The test must be carried out on devices of various types. In order not to be distracted by opening access to the site and using real devices, you can change the width of the browser window. The effect will be the same.
2. You must check the home page, category page, post page, and offline page. If you plan to create tags and connect them to publications, then you need to check the tag page. You should also check the search results page.
3. Check the general appearance of the pages. Elements and blocks must be positioned in accordance with the templates and settings made. When you change the screen width or use different types of devices, the page layout should change to match the settings for those devices. Parts of pages should not overlap each other or fit tightly together unless this is intended.
4. Check the behavior of the header on different types of devices. Pay attention to the opening and closing of the main menu panel on mobile devices.
5. Check the appearance of the page content. Pay attention to the font sizes of headings and body text. Headings should be sized so that they do not take up too much space or be split into too many lines on devices with small screen widths. The size and color of the main text should ensure easy reading and high contrast.
6. Test the appearance and behavior of footer elements at different screen widths. Pay attention to the size and contrast of fonts. It is also very important that on phone and tablet screens when the footer content is converted into a vertical structure, the alignment of the text in the footer blocks looks logical.
7. Check that the width of page elements does not exceed the width of the pages, especially on mobile devices. This is important not only for the convenience of users but also for good ranking in search engines - a search bot considers such a flaw a rather serious mistake. For example, if the category name is a very long word, then the width of the menu item on a mobile device may be larger than the width of the screen. Graphics, comment form elements, footer widgets, search fields - all this also requires checking.
8. If everything is good and you have nothing else to complain about, then just see what can be improved without redoing everything that has already been done. After all, your personal satisfaction with the work you do is just as important as anything else, right?
9. Write down all your comments, go back to tweaking the theme and CSS, and just correct everything on the list.

4.8.3. What Needs to Be Done Later

You, of course, already understood that we have not considered all the possibilities and solved not all the problems associated with customizing the appearance of the site.

This is due to the fact that we have not yet structured the site - we have not created a category system, set up a menu, created tags, and linked them to publications. We will consider structuring issues in the next chapter, and visualize the menu and tags - when preparing the site for opening, when it is already filled with a sufficient amount of content.

In addition, there are elements such as the site logo. You, of course, expect us to resolve this issue as well. So it will be. And also when preparing the site for opening.

Why haven't we resolved these issues now? The main task was to learn how to customize the appearance of the site, and we learned how to do it. And it took a lot of time and even more patience. We will solve specific problems as they arise.

Here is a list of what needs to be created to make the site look finished.

1. Menu system. First of all, there is the main menu, which mainly consists of categories. An additional menu, which consists of links to mandatory and simply necessary pages of the site.
2. External links. Here we will need widgets dedicated to this, social network icons, and links to external services if provided.
3. Tag cloud - general for the site, and lists of tags for posts.
4. The main site icon, which is attached to the browser tab and can be used in other places, such as the phone screen when installing PWA.
5. The site logo, which is located in the header, and fits well into the design of the pages.
6. A version of the site logo that is intended specifically for use in search results and must meet special requirements.

We will solve all these problems by the time the site opens.

Stage Results

We have passed a very large, labor-intensive, and important stage. Website design is what everyone sees, what everyone talks about, what everyone argues about, what is very easy to criticize, and what can be difficult to be proud of.

Not all website design tasks have been completed yet. To be honest, they can never be completely resolved, because you will always have a desire to improve, refine and redo something.

Luckily, you now have enough knowledge to do everything we just listed. You have learned a lot, learned a lot, seen a lot and, I hope, you have already tried to do a lot on your own.

We learned what you need to pay attention to when choosing a theme, what you need to do before installing it, installed the theme, and checked how the site looks right after installing it.

We learned what is needed to create a child theme, created, installed, and successfully activated it.

We studied a large and complex system of settings for all elements of website pages using the example of a truly modern and high-quality block theme. We went through all the visual components of the pages and understood how to customize their appearance.

We learned what *CSS* technology is for, how it can be practically used when customizing a website design, and customized the appearance of several real-life elements.

We saw how a classic theme differs from a block theme, learned how to customize it, and understood what features and advantages it has.

We checked the appearance of the site's pages, visually assessed its changes for different types of devices, and found out which tasks that were related to the site's design had not been resolved at this stage.

We will begin to solve these problems at the next stage, and this will be the stage of structuring the site.

As always, write down everything you've done in the Planner.

5

Structuring
the WordPress Website

Stage Tasks

We are starting the fifth stage of work on the site. At this stage, we have to start making the site meaningful. We will need to make it clear and convenient for the visitor.

A website visitor should understand at first glance where he is and what he sees in front of him. The visitor should feel comfortable and interact with the site in a way that is convenient for him and how we need it.

Here, we come closest to what experts denote by the abbreviations *UI/UX*. No matter how elegant and beautiful the website interface may be, without interaction with the visitor, it is of no value.

We need to give the user the ability to interact with the site. This does not mean that the site interface should be filled with various exciting controls that blink invitingly, recolor, and change shape and size, prompting the user to move, press, rotate, and switch something. There is nothing wrong with all this if it can really help to captivate the visitor.

The most important thing that can captivate a visitor is the correctly presented information that he was looking for and the opportunity to take the actions that he intended to take.

For the visitor to receive all this, all information on the site must be correctly structured, ordered, and presented.

For the visitor to see the information, it must be in the places where he will look for it. To do this, you need to visually structure information blocks and website elements in a logical sequence and expected combinations.

For the visitor to quickly find what he needs, he needs to be allowed to access large arrays of thematically homogeneous publications quickly. To do this, we need to create a simple, understandable, and convenient system of categories and tags.

For the visitor to perform a minimum of actions to find the necessary information, a simple and understandable menu system, a tag cloud located in a convenient place, and other navigation elements are required.

It is also necessary that the site contains the necessary pages with official information, which the visitor can also find easily and quickly.

And finally, there is one category of *VIP* visitors that you need to keep in mind at all times. We mean search engine bots. They also know how to evaluate the structure of a site and do so, and the results of such an assessment will certainly be taken into account when determining the quality of the site and its position in search results.

And finally, you need to check how it all turned out - check everything without leaving out any details. Check everything from the home page to the various must-have official information pages. I hope I managed to scare you just enough (and by no means more) that you decided to start structuring your site immediately. We'll start by learning something useful about the internal structure of the site.

5.1. Internal Structure of the Website

5.1.1. Internal Structure of the Website and Its Appearance

There is a point of view that the internal structure of the site - categories and navigation system - and its external structure - that is, how it looks, are related but different things.

This view of things is inherent in *UI/UX* specialists, marketers, designers, and, in general, all technical specialists who are accustomed to filling the term "usability" with a meaning they understand.

It's not hard to guess that all these wonderful people know how to solve narrow problems professionally, but none of them are obliged to delve into the intricacies and meanings of your business. Yes, you most likely won't tell any of them everything.

A marketer may be closest to the truth, but he is not required to be able to solve all the problems of website structuring. Therefore, the role of the site owner at this stage is the most important and most important.

It is most reasonable to approach this role with the understanding that the external, visible structure of the site is just a reflection, or visualization, of what is actually on the site - its content and internal structure.

After all, it's stupid to add items with catchy names to the menu if there is no place on the site where they could lead, right? And it is no less unreasonable to hide deep into the navigation system something that the visitor absolutely must see as soon as possible.

In any case, the visitor's expectations should not be deceived, and content plays a major role in this. It is the content that we ultimately structure. A bit unclear? No problem. By the end of this chapter, you will wonder how something so obvious never occurred to you before.

When you then look at competitors' sites, you will see that many of them succeeded in understanding structuring issues and found elegant solutions, and many could not do this, although it would seem so simple! So, the external structure of the site reflects its internal structure. Form is a consequence of content, and not vice versa.

5.1.2. What are Taxonomies

The internal structure includes taxonomies. What is this, you ask?

Taxonomy is a characteristic or property by which content is classified.

Taxonomies do not exist separately from a specific type of content. Using a taxonomy, or more precisely, using a specific object related to a specific taxonomy, content units that are associated with this object are grouped.

Unclear? It's okay; we'll now clarify the situation with an example. You will understand everything, and then everything will be completely clear (Figure 5.1).

Such a universally understandable piece of content as the post "*The most beautiful flowers in my garden*" can be tied to a specific "*Flowers*" category. A unit of content is a post, a taxonomy is categories, and a post is tied to one of the categories.

You can link a post to several categories, but one of them must be "canonical," that is, the main one, and search engines must know about it; otherwise, such a post will end up in a search ban because the search bot will find the same content at different addresses (*URL*).

Another well-known taxonomy is tags. The same post can be linked to the tags "*orchids*," "*roses*," and "*daisies*."

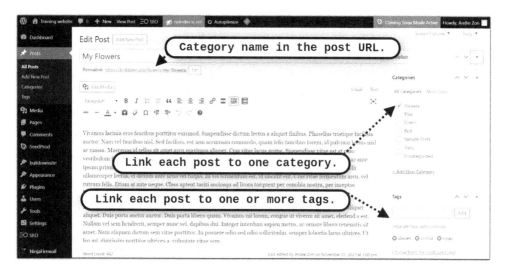

Figure 5-1. Linking a post to a category and tags.

You can attach several tags to one post, and this will not lead to any consequences because tags do not participate in the formation of addresses (*URLs*).

Are there other taxonomies besides categories and tags?

Yes, they do exist. There are two more standard classic *WordPress* taxonomies - link categories and post types (formats). They are quite rarely used, are not taken into account by search engines, are not used for navigation, and we will not consider them.

In order not to leave this question completely unanswered, let's say a few words about them. The post format can be set when creating and editing it. Some themes use this information to make different types of posts look different and generally stand out from the general background of the site. This taxonomy has no further use.

Link categories have nothing to do with post categories. Once upon a time, before *WordPress 3.5*, links were an independent and quite important type of content. Therefore, for the convenience of working with them, it was customary to classify them. This is exactly what this taxonomy was used for.

Now, it only makes sense to use it if you are really dealing with a large number of links. But for this to be possible, you will have to make additional efforts - this functionality is not included by default in modern versions of *WordPress*.

It should be said that this is not all. *WordPress* provides technology for creating your own taxonomies. This is not a task for beginners or even advanced website owners. This is already a professional level, and such a need arises when solving problems for which there are no ready-made solutions in the form of themes or plugins.

For such work, you need to have a good knowledge of the *PHP* programming language and be able to work with it. You need to know the *WordPress* structure well and understand what is written in the "*WordPress code.*" All this is beyond the scope of our plans and, therefore, is not considered here. We already have a lot of work ahead of us.

So, we have two types of taxonomies at our disposal: categories and tags.

This is not the site structure yet but only a tool for creating it. We already know enough about taxonomies to use this tool for its intended purpose to form the structure of the site.

Our training website has a very simple structure. There are only a few posts on it that are completely abstract in content. We will artificially complicate it - we will create several categories and tags. When we finish this work, you will understand how you need to structure the posts on your site. When work is underway to create not a training but a real site, categories and tags need to be planned and created first.

5.2. Creating Categories

5.2.1. Number and Nesting of Categories

Creating categories is a fairly simple job. But to do it correctly, you need to have some knowledge. You need to know the answers to questions that are not always obvious and some are little known. We will answer all these questions right now, during our practical work on the training site. The first of these questions is how many categories do you need?

There is no short answer to this question. More exactly to say, there are several important considerations to keep in mind instead of the direct answer.

Often, the main menu of a site contains all created categories, but this is entirely optional. Of course, full compliance of the menu and categories of the site simplifies the life of the site owner and does not leave any ambiguities for visitors. Maybe the site needs categories that will be accessible using special widgets or some bright buttons. It depends on the theme and objectives of the site.

On our training site, we will create three categories that we will call "*Red*", "*Green*", and "*Blue*" (Figure 5.2). In the future, they will form the basis of the main menu of the site.

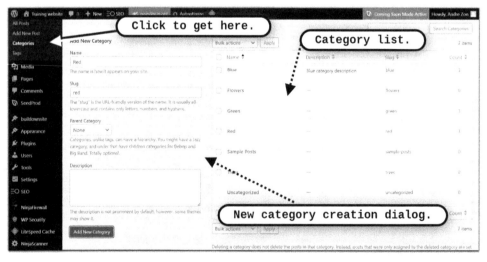

Figure 5-2. Categories/ Add New Category page: creating a category.

In the Red category, create a nested Dark Red category (Figure 5.3).

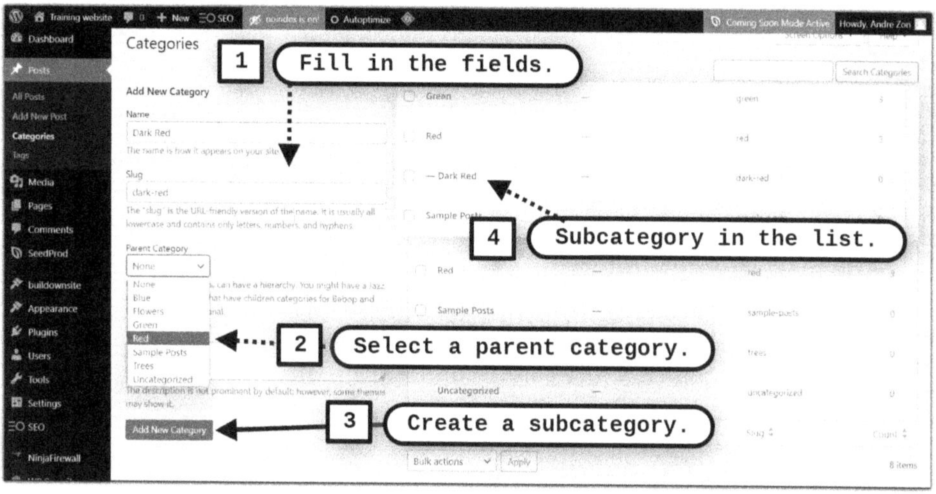

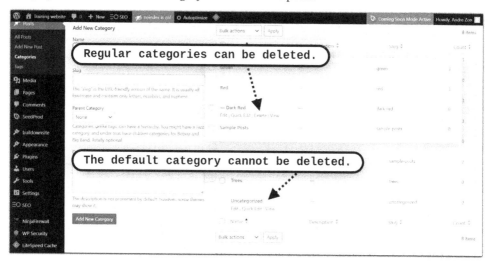

Figure 5-3. Categories/ Add New Category page: creating a nested category.

It is not recommended to create more than two levels of categories. The more levels of nesting of categories, the worse the pages that are linked to the lowest level categories will be indexed by search engines.

Pay attention to the "*Uncategorized*" category (Figure 5.4). This is a category that *WordPress* creates automatically, and this category cannot be deleted. You can edit it, rename it, and do whatever you want with it, but you cannot delete it. The fact is that this category is set as the default category for created site posts.

Figure 5-4. Categories/ "Uncategorized" category as default.

We can change the default category (Figure 5.5), as you remember, on the *Settings/ Writing* page. Let's set "*Red*" as the default category.

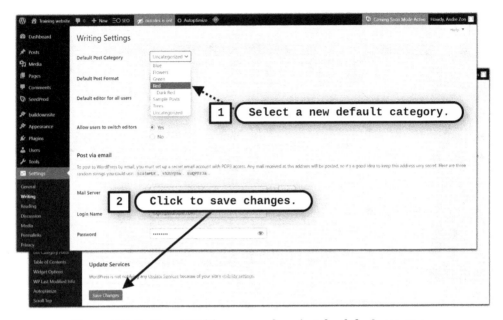

Figure 5-5. Settings/ Writing page: changing the default category.

Let's go back to the categories page. Now, the "*Uncategorized*" category can be removed, but the "*Red*" category cannot (Figure 5.6).

By the way, here's what needs to be said about the "default category."

The "default category" is needed only to ensure that the created posts do not end up being unrelated to any category. If this were to happen, the site's structure, based on the usage of the taxonomy of categories, would be destroyed. Therefore, when you create, save as a draft, or publish a post and do not specify which category it should be assigned to, the post is automatically assigned to the "default category."

Figure 5-6. Categories/ "Uncategorized" category removing.

This allows you to avoid destroying the integrity of the site structure, but be careful! Each post at the time of publication must be assigned to the desired category and not to the "default category."

Every post for which you do not do this will end up in the search engine index as being in the "default category" in the literal sense. And then you will have to correct your mistake for many weeks or even months. So be very careful... or change the "default category" to a meaningful option, as shown above.

5.2.2. The Importance of Correctly Linking Posts to Categories

For you to better understand the importance of correctly linking posts to categories, we will add a little and clarify what you just read above.

When creating posts, you should always explicitly set a category and carefully control this process, even if the "default category" is correctly set in accordance with the tasks and thematics of your website.

If you perform publication carelessly and a post is mistakenly assigned to the default category, a search engine bot may index the resulting *URL*, and correcting the assigning of a post to another category will inevitably lower its search rankings.

5.2.3. How to Create Categories Correctly

The order in which categories are created does not matter. Search engine bots do not take it into account when indexing posts and the location of categories in the menu is not related to the sequence in which they were created.

Therefore, just create them in such an order that it is convenient to work with their list when editing. This list (Figure 5.7) cannot be sorted by date - only by title, description, slug, and number of linked posts.

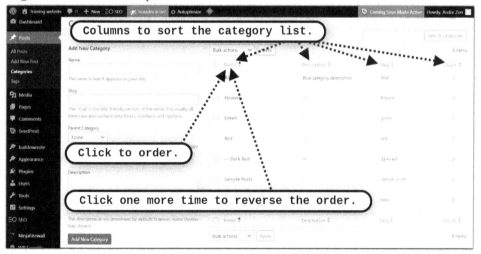

Figure 5-7. Categories page: a list of website categories.

The length of a *"category name"* field often raises questions. A title that is too long can cause the menu to extend beyond the screen's width on phones. The long category name is also inconvenient when viewing the site on a computer when the menu items are located horizontally.

Let's take a closer look at the category editing page (Fig. 5.8).

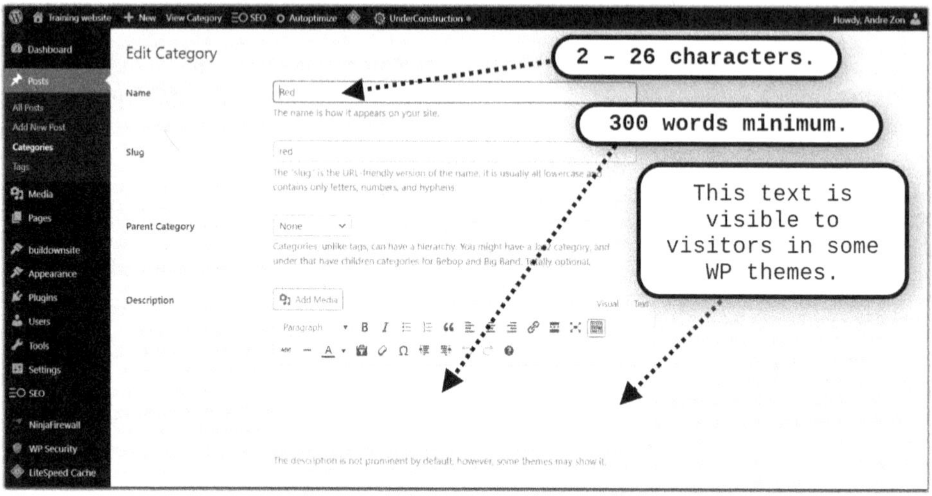

Figure 5-8. Edit Category page.

Even more inconvenient is when the category name consists of more than one word, and the visitor will have to guess where one menu item ends and the next one begins.

At the same time, there is no special restriction on the length of the category name. The rule of thumb that website developers follow is very simple: 2 to 26 characters, and no more! In general, there is nothing unexpected here.

It is customary to write category names in lowercase letters and start the first word with a capital letter, as in sentences. If necessary, using *CSS* you can configure the display of category names in different places in different ways. For example, in the menu - no changes, but in the widget with links - in capital letters. Of course, for it, you do not need to change the category names using editing. *CSS* can do this, as we already know.

Here, we need to say a few words about what a "*slug*" is. Slug is the *URL*-friendly equivalent of a category name. Slug will become part of not only the category *URL*, but also the URLs of all posts that are included in this category. Therefore, it is highly desirable, and even necessary, for the slug to be at least a keyword. If a slug is required to be more than one word, then only the hyphen character is required and permitted to be used as a delimiter.

Here, we first encountered this question, but you should understand and remember well: the only separator that search engines correctly understand is the hyphen!

If your *URL* contains several keywords, do not merge them into one word, but separate them with a hyphen! The underscore sign should not be used - it is the equivalent of gluing words together rather than separating them. Only a sign of a hyphen! Then, search engines will understand everything correctly, and this will have a positive effect on search results.

And one more thing: slug, like the rest of the *URL*, should not contain anything other than lowercase letters of the basic Latin alphabet, numbers, and hyphens! This rule is always true.

There is also a standard field called "*category description*". Why is this description needed at all if all that is required from the category is a name and a link in the main menu of the site? Not so simple! There are at least two reasons why category description matters.

Firstly, some themes provide category descriptions on their main pages of categories itself. By using such themes, you can give site visitors more information about what's contained in a category and allow search engines to index categories and include them in search results.

Secondly, there is an additional opportunity to promote the site on social networks. If the category has its own description, is also prepared for *SEO*, and contains all the necessary meta tags, then it can be shared on social networks, such as a regular post or page. Few people think about this possibility, and in vain. A great opportunity! And it needs to be used.

The length of the visible category description has no special restrictions.

Create a description that meets user expectations and truly describes the category's content.

Focus on the volume of a regular small post. Looking ahead a little, I will say: 300 words constitute the required *SEO* minimum, starting from which search engines pay (or rather, can pay) attention to any text.

Now, do you think we have figured out everything about the categories, their names, and descriptions?

No, that wasn't all. We talked about the visible title and the category visible description and also found out what a slug is and what it should be.

We also mentioned *SEO* for categories. Now, we need to add a little information about this.

5.2.4. SEO for Categories

Look at the *SEO* settings block on the category editing page (Fig. 5.9). There are fields here for title and description options that will never be displayed on the site but will become meta tags. This is valuable information for both search engines and social networks.

But for social networks, the *SEO* plugin also provides options for titles and descriptions! Add them, and they will go into the category page codes that meet *Facebook* and *Twitter* requirements and are the standard for everyone else.

And one more thing: Please note that here, you can add illustrations that will be displayed in your social network feed when you share a category there, like a regular post.

What do you think about the opportunity to attract additional attention to your site - whether it should be ignored? It's definitely a must-use!

Now you know almost everything about categories, and it's time to start talking about tags.

5.3. Creating Tags

5.3.1. Differences Between Tags and Categories

We've already briefly discussed the differences between tags and categories, although their behavior is very similar. When visiting a category page, a visitor sees posts that are associated with it. When visiting a tag page, a visitor also sees posts that are associated with it.

What is the point of creating tags? And is it necessary to create them if the site already has categories?

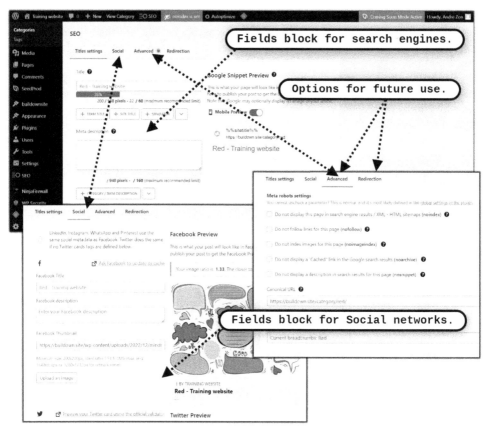

Figure 5-9. Edit Category page/ SEO metabox.

First, pay attention to this (Fig. 5.10). The name of the category, or rather the ee slug, is always contained in the full *URL* of each post that belongs to this category.

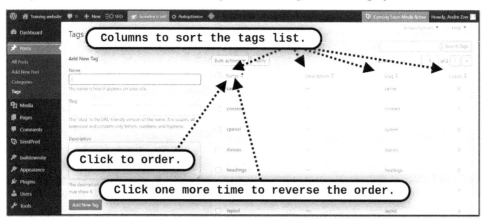

Figure 5-10. Tags page: a list of website tags.

The title, or slug, of a tag, is never part of the full *URL* of any post on the entire site.

The tag name is included only in the *URL* of the tag page itself. This page contains a summary of all posts associated with this tag. When navigating to any of these posts, the *URL* that includes the category is always used, and the *URL* that includes the tag name is never used.

It turns out that a category is a taxonomy that is involved in creating the structure of the site. Is a tag a dead-end taxonomy that only generates pages of the tags themselves? That is how it is.

Then why do we need tags?

There are three fundamental reasons for this.

Firstly, if your site contains posts on different topics, then it will be challenging for you to fit them all into a category system (and menu). In addition, very often, it is necessary to focus the visitor's attention on something more specific and memorable than the meaning of the category name. Using a combination of categories and tags, you give the content semantic order.

Secondly, a tag cloud, if you approach its creation correctly, can significantly help the visitor navigate the site.

In addition to the menu and search, the visitor gets access to a very visual and straightforward tool for quickly jumping to publications on the topic he needs. As a result, the visitor will view and read more publications and spend more time on your site, seeing more banners and offers.

This will not only increase the average return on site visits. There is something else very important - and this is the next reason.

Thirdly, the longer the average time a visitor spends on a site and the more actions he or she performs, such as paging, scrolling, and clicking on navigation elements, the higher his or her engagement rate. And this is very important from the point of view of search engines!

You will be surprised, but behavioral characteristics often mean no less to the success of a website than *SEO*. And such characteristics can be perfectly measured by the system with which you will inevitably deal.

We mean, of course, the *Google Analytics* system.

Simply put, failure to use or ineffective use of tags harms a site by worsening its behavioral characteristics and reducing the average revenue per visitor.

Now, let's talk about how this is done. Adding and editing tags is very similar to working with categories we just learned (Fig. 5.11). Therefore, we will not repeat ourselves; we will only note the features and differences.

5.3.2. How to Create Tags Correctly

The tag length should, on average, be shorter than the length of the category name. This is because the tag cloud is rarely located horizontally. The usual place for its placement is a narrow sidebar or one of the footer columns. Long tags will deform the layout, and a cloud consisting of long tags will take up too much space vertically on the page. From 3 to 8 characters is the optimal tag length.

Lowercase letters are traditionally used for tags. This is optional. It's just that if a tag cloud consists of tags starting with capital letters, then such a cloud, oddly enough, becomes less readable. Of course, if the tag is an abbreviation, then it is better to write such a tag in all capital letters.

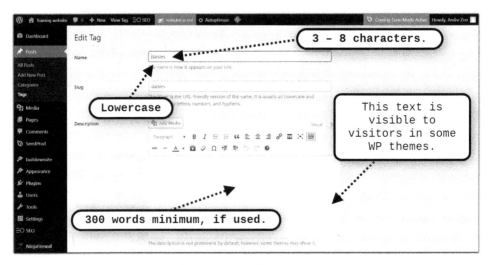

Figure 5-11. Edit Tag page.

You may find it strange that starting tags with capital letters is not a good idea. After all, a capital letter at the beginning of a word should attract attention and indicate the beginning of the tag, thereby helping the visitor navigate the cloud!

Yes, that happens. But to do this, the theme you use on the site should not highlight tags in other ways. However, such methods exist, and they are also traditional.

The first way is to change the font size depending on the frequency of use of the tag on the site. Very clear and intuitive! This technique always helps to solve the problem of visual localization of a tag cloud on a website by its visitor. Otherwise, the tag cloud may simply get lost among other widgets. Some themes use this technique very well, and some don't.

The second method is to highlight the background of each tag separately. This method completely solves the problem of separating tags from each other and makes the tag cloud stand out well among other widgets.

Some themes use the first or second method, and some themes use both methods at the same time.

Our tutorial site doesn't have many tags, so we can't see it all in an impressive enough way. But you should already be aware that using a capital letter at the beginning of a tag contradicts traditional ways of highlighting tags in the cloud and neutralizes their effect. The cloud becomes challenging to read and looks somewhat sloppy.

However, it is possible that this will not be the case for the theme you choose for your site. The final decision is yours.

Of course, similar to the case with categories, using *CSS*, you can configure the display of tags in different places in different ways. Of course, there must be some reasons for this.

The number of tags, as well as categories, is not explicitly limited in any way. But while you can decide for yourself which categories to include in menus or widgets, that's not the case with the tag cloud. It always includes all the tags that you created and attached to posts. Therefore, when determining the number of tags and their composition, remember that the tag cloud should fit well into the site page layout and not take up too much space on it.

5.3.3. Attaching Tags to Posts and Their Place on the Website

You can attach an arbitrary number of tags to a post. You need to be guided only by considerations of meaning and convenience.

You can also pay attention to the placement of post-related tags on the post page. They are usually located below the post text. Just control the appearance of this sequence of tags so that it does not disrupt the overall aesthetics of the page if this is important to your site.

Tag pages are often not included in the sitemap and are not intended to be indexed by search engines. But, as you may already have guessed, this does not guarantee they will not be indexed.

Therefore, similar to what was discussed for categories, do not neglect the opportunity to use keywords important to the site first for tags and create an indexable description for them.

If your theme supports displaying descriptions on tag pages, you can give visitors and search engines more information about your site.

5.3.4. SEO for Tags

Don't miss the opportunity to fill out all the *SEO* fields for tags and include all the necessary information for social media meta tags (Fig. 5.12). If you use all these opportunities, then you will be able to use tags, as well as categories, to promote your site on social networks.

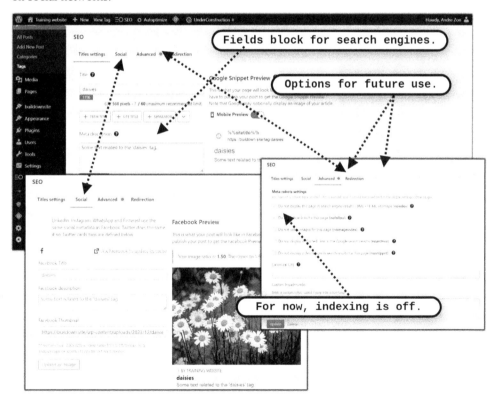

Figure 5-12. Edit Tag page/ SEO metabox.

Just fill out all the fields the *SEO* plugin provides for the tag - and you can share the tags on social networks like regular posts!

Advice for the future. Descriptions and tag titles do not have to be identical to *SEO* descriptions and titles. Descriptions and titles for *SEO* do not have to be the same as descriptions and titles for social media meta tags. Moreover, it will be much better if they are all different from each other.

The fact is that *SEO* meta tags are used to display information about a site in search engines. Therefore, when creating *SEO* versions of titles and descriptions, it is best to try to tell the user something more exciting and call-to-action than competitors are doing. This is information for search results!

The content of meta tags for social networks is what users of those networks will see. When preparing these meta tags, you can take into account the specifics of these networks, expectations, and even the vocabulary of the audience, and this is correct. This is information for them.

We have finished studying categories and tags. They are needed when publishing and structuring not all content but only part of it - posts. The other part is stand-alone pages, which are not tied to categories or associated with tags. Let's work with them.

5.4. Adding Required Pages

5.4.1. About Using Pages

If you have such a desire, then you can probably find several plugins in the *WordPress* repository that will allow you to link pages with categories and tags. I've dealt with sites that needed this. But this is such a rarity that it is impossible to talk about it as a general need. Pages are designed to be self-contained. They are purposed to do things that are not possible within the standard post page template. Now, have you noticed the confusion? There is a page - and there is a post page. How do we understand what is at stake in each specific case? It makes most sense to call a "post page" a "post" and mean a "post" that can be viewed on the site with its own *URL* (Fig. 5.13).

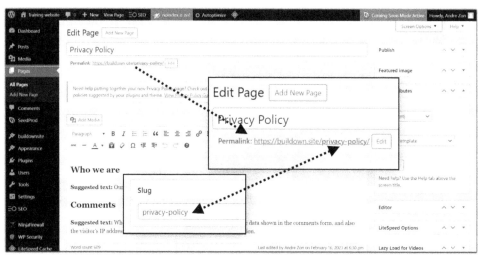

Figure 5-13. The Page URL example.

Everything that we see around the post itself, and with which it forms a page, is just a template. A special type of page template that is always used when publishing a post.

A standalone published page, or simply "page," is never used as a template. It exists on its own and does not require attachment to a category. Therefore, its URL does not include anything extra - only the base *URL* of the site and the slug of the page itself.

The Posts are made on a conveyor belt.

The Pages are handmade.

All they have in common is the header and footer. There may also be a sidebar, but it is not at all necessary and is not always needed.

Posts always contain content related to the category topic and basic interactive elements, such as social sharing buttons. Pages logically relate to the entire site and can contain any content and any interactive elements.

Pages have yet another purpose. Pages can be used as templates for the "home page" and, with some themes and plugins, as "category pages." The first case is quite standard, and we will briefly consider it, but the second is too special, and we will not consider it. We already have a lot of less exotic work to do besides that.

The main typical work with pages on any site is to create a set of mandatory pages that contain mostly formal information.

Different countries and even different states have quite varied requirements for this information, but there is a lot in common.

When you create actual pages, keep this in mind. You may need legal advice, especially if you are creating a website for a company or if your website topic requires official licensing.

The "*About*" page is the first thing that comes to mind, right?

5.4.2. "About" Page

That's what could be going on here. Visitors may be interested in anything they can think of. Therefore, you need to first keep in mind those visitors who you need most.

If you sell your expert services and products, tell them about your experience.

If you sell products, tell them what properties of the products make your offerings unique.

If you are looking for cooperation, tell them what you need and what you can offer to possible partners.

Write about the main thing for the main part of your target audience!

If your site is a blog that involves showcasing your activities, home, work, travel, or hobbies, then you need to provide information about yourself that may be relevant to any subject of the above.

If your site is a resource of expert information or a source of special professional knowledge, then information about yourself should contain a minimum of personal information and one or two paragraphs of information about your professional experience and your qualifications.

The third block of information is official. If you are required by law to disclose information about the owner or administrator of the site, do so here, and be sure to add information about what law you are doing this under.

Nothing else is needed on this page. Of course, you can add something else. We simply cannot provide for all options here.

5.4.3. "Privacy Policy" Page

"*Privacy Policy*" is the most official, most formal, and most mandatory page of the site. After installation, *WordPress* will offer you a template for this page. By default, the page is called "P*rivacy Policy*" and has the slug "*privacy-policy*." It is better to leave this information unchanged.

This page template is quite functional, but it is short and will not always be enough.

It is best to place the following information on this page:

- information about the information collected about users, its composition, and subsequent use (if you collect this information) or that the site does not use such information,
- information about whether your site offers the creation of personal user accounts and about the composition and nature of the use of the account information provided by users (hint: if you have such a need, pay attention to plugins that allow you to use social network accounts to log into the site),
- information about whether your site allows comments on posts and how you will store and use comment content and information about their authors,
- information about what information about users is stored in the server logs, and when, how, and in what cases it can be used (hint: a visitor's *IP* address can, for example, be banned if attempts are made to hack the site using this address),
- information about what types of cookies the site uses and for what purposes this is done.

If a mobile application is associated with your site, then you should write a separate "Privacy Policy" page for this application or add a special, properly named block of information to the page that we just talked about.

5.4.4. "Terms and Conditions" Page

"*Terms and conditions*" are exactly what should be here. The visitor needs to be explained how to behave on the site and talk about mutual obligations. Here's the best way to do it.

1. Introductory block. Here, you need to formally notify the visitor of the need to read and follow the rules for using the site and that if he disagrees with the rules, he must leave the site. This is an official point that can always be referred to if the need arises.
2. Block of information about the content of the site. Here, you need to tell what content is posted on the site, where you got it and, how you created it, who owns the rights to texts, images, videos, and other types of content. It is also necessary to communicate what the user has the right to do with the content and what not. Since we assume that you only publish your own content on the site, we also assume that, in this case, you yourself determine the boundaries of what you are allowed to do.
3. If applicable, here you can also indicate a formal method of communication with the copyright holder, that is, with you. If you use the services of content protection companies, please also provide information about this.
4. A block of information about the accuracy and reliability of published information. Here you need to describe the nature of the information - entertainment, reference, educational, and so on. You also need to indicate what

level of depth and expertise this information corresponds to - personal impressions, observations, professional analysis, expert recommendations, etc. The site visitor should respect your work, but he should not be misled. Therefore, write honestly about the degree of reliability and accuracy of publications you can provide. Don't be ashamed of your unprofessionalism; it will be much worse if you don't report it on time, but someone else catches you in it.

5. You can also place the official *Disclaimer* here. This is almost always necessary. Even if you publish information whose absolute safety has been verified throughout human history, you still officially disclaim responsibility for the consequences of its use by anyone. And also refuse responsibility for not using this information. Any adult who understands the nature and possible results of any legal disputes will definitely tell you that it is best not to get involved in them. This is exactly what *Disclaimer* is for.

5.4.5. "Contacts" page

"*Contacts*" is the shortest of the required pages.

Here, you can place a form for sending a letter. This form can be easily created using a special plugin and can be done later when the site is almost ready to open.

Here, you can also publish a list of links to your pages and profiles on social networks, instant messengers, and trading systems.

Please note that in some countries, there is a requirement to disclose full official contact information, especially if you are not acting as an individual but as an entrepreneur or on behalf of a company. If this is your case, then this page should contain such information.

5.4.6. Additional Tips by Pages

We recommend that you include at the end of each required page the date it was last updated and notice that you reserve the right to make changes.

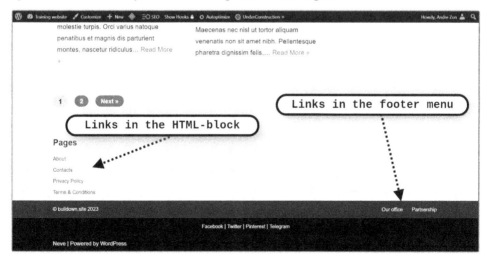

Figure 5-14. Links to obligatory pages in the footer menu.

It should be borne in mind that such pages are required not only because they inspire the respect and trust of the user but also because they are simply necessary by legal requirements.

If your site does not have such pages, then you will not be able to take advantage of commercial opportunities to promote it on some popular platforms.

Therefore, treat the creation of such pages responsibly and ensure they are up to date.

If you're still feeling unsure about creating and formatting their content, just create these pages, give them the right names, and add links to them, e.g., in the footer menu (Fig. 5.14).

Simply save the intended content as text files on your computer. You will be able to complete this work after we have covered all the issues related to content creation.

Required pages must be available throughout the site. This is usually done, as we just said, using link widgets and a menu system. It is the menu settings that we will now deal with.

5.5. Setting Up Menus

5.5.1. What are Menus and How to Use Them

In the most general sense, a menu is simply a compact block of links that are stylistically combined into a visually localizable and recognizable object.

Unlike other types of link blocks, the classic menu works like a toggle.

This means that if you click on one of the items, then after clicking on the associated link, this item becomes inactive and, in appearance, may differ from other active items in the same menu (or may not differ; this is a matter of taste and design).

Depending on the structure, volume, purpose, and tasks of the site, an arbitrary number of different menus can be used on it.

It should be noted that there are established stereotypes in this matter, which are determined by traditions and correspond to visitors' expectations. Therefore, being too original in creating a menu system can do more harm than good.

Using a menu is utterly optional if your website is a landing page or a personal business card and there are no publications on it.

If you have a thematic or informational site and publications are tied to categories, then you need to use the menu.

Even if you don't want to do this or for some reason you don't like hearing the word "menu" itself, you will still have to create, configure, and place at least one menu on the site.

This is what visitors expect; it helps them navigate the site, and any WordPress theme has everything you need for this.

The *Appearance/Menus* page (Fig. 5.15) is used to configure menu composition and assign different locations to them.

Menu advanced properties are configured on the *Appearance/ Customize/ Menus* pages (Fig. 5.16).

For different themes, approximately the same approach is used: menu composition and placement binding are done on one page, and behaviour and appearance settings are done on another.

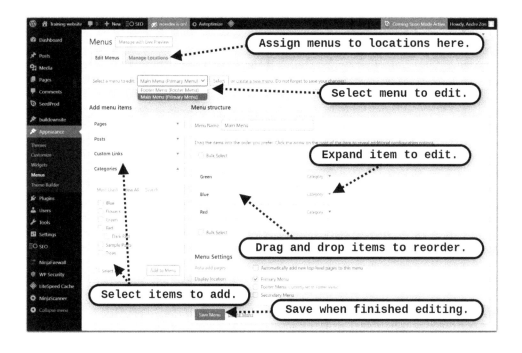

Figure 5-15. Appearance/ Menus page.

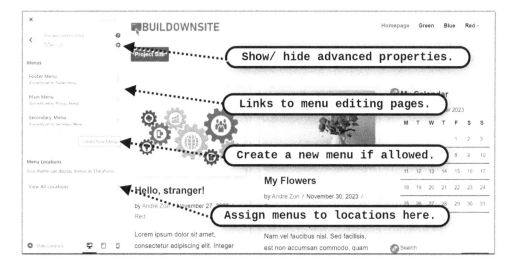

Figure 5-16. Appearance/ Customize/ Menus page.

5.5.2. Main Menu

If you have a small website and are not active on social networks, then just one menu may be enough for you.

This menu is usually called the main menu and includes links to site categories (Fig. 5.17).

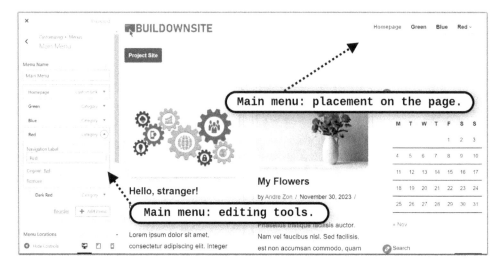

Figure 5-17. Appearance/ Customize/ Menus/ Main Menu page.

There are no mandatory requirements for the main menu. The categories in it can be arranged in any order that you deem correct.

In addition to categories, the menu may include links to some pages of the site that you consider worthy of it. For example, this could be a page with answers to questions, a landing page for collecting leads, a showcase of your products and services, or something else.

Very often, the first item in the main menu is traditionally a link to the homepage of the site.

The main menu is an important and basic navigation tool not only for people but also for search bots.

Both of them don't like it if the main menu, in addition to the top level, has more than one nested level.

Therefore, if you have a large and thematically diverse website, its structure needs to be built in with a minimum number of levels of nesting of categories.

5.5.3. Mobile Menu and Secondary Menu

A mobile menu is simply a version of the main menu that is designed to be displayed on mobile devices and specifically adapted for them.

When to display this version is decided by the theme installed on the site. When setting it up, you can visually control this on the Appearance/ Header & Footer page.

Why can or should the mobile version of the main menu differ from the desktop version? Is this necessary?

Not always. Here are the reasons that matter:

- the categories have long names, and you agree to make them shorter in the mobile menu only because they do not fit in width, and in the main version of the main menu, it is crucial for you to leave them as they are,
- due to the nature of the template, the names of nested categories are displayed with a more noticeable indentation and do not fit in width, so it is better to move them to the same level as the higher categories,
- not all categories or pages of the site are needed by mobile users or are simply not designed to work on mobile devices, and they need to be excluded from the mobile menu,
- some categories or pages are designed only to work on mobile devices, and they need to be included in the mobile version of the main menu and excluded from the main version.
-

A handy feature. Unfortunately, not all themes support mobile menus.

Our theme does not support it because it generates the main menu for mobile devices automatically.

But our theme has a Secondary Menu (Fig. 5.18).

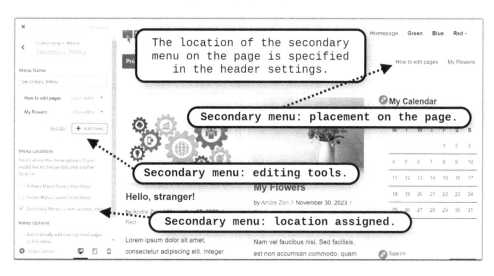

Figure 5-18. Appearance/ Menus/ Secondary Menu page.

Surely it can be useful if the site has a complex structure.

In terms of its capabilities, it is no different from the main menu and can also be located anywhere in the header.

We'll just put the same categories there as in the main menu to see how it looks.

5.5.4. Footer Menu

The menu in the footer (Fig. 5.19) is usually used to place links to mandatory and official pages of the site.

This menu does not attract attention and is used by those visitors who really need information about the site.

We will do the same and add links to formal pages to the footer menu.

If the theme you are using does not have a menu in the footer, then it can be replaced with a widget with links, which can also be placed in the footer.

At the right time, we will make such a widget so that you have a ready-made example.

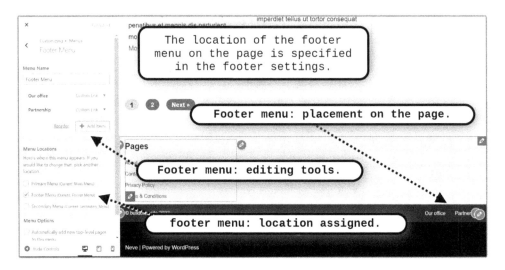

Figure 5-19. Appearance/ Menus/ Footer Menu page.

5.5.5. Social Menu

This type of menu is not directly related to the site. Social menu items contain links to your pages and profiles on social networks, instant messengers, bookmarking services, and other similar places.

In most cases, if the theme supports this type of menu, individual social networks and other services correspond to ready-made icons that are embedded in the theme and coordinated with the rest of the theme's design elements.

If the theme does not support the social menu, and you need to use it, then the plugin will help solve the problem.

There are many plugins of this kind, and even in free versions, you can often find everything you need.

But the best way is to add a widget to the footer with links to your pages and profiles. Why?

Here are the reasons:

- the plugin may not contain icons for all social networks,
- the plugins do not provide the ability to add more than one icon for the same social network (for example, if you need to specify not only a page but also a Facebook group),
- social network icons are decorative but not informative - there is no way to

indicate where exactly the icon leads (group, page, personal profile, and so on),
* the layout of a group of icons is difficult or impossible to manage if there are a lot of icons (the plugin can automatically move icons that do not fit, for example, in the sidebar),
* plugins offer a limited number of icon design options, which may not suit your site in color, size, or shape.

In addition, the plugin, of course, can slow down your site.

The custom widget is free of all these shortcomings.

It is not so decorative because it consists only of texts, but it does not limit us in any way to the rest (Fig. 5.20).

Such a widget can be easily created similarly to the widget for the formal pages of the site, which we talked about a little earlier. We will make both widgets when preparing the site for opening.

Of course, it is possible that some plugin may be, nevertheless, useful for your site.

We discussed everything related to the menu and link system, made menu options for the test site, and postponed working with link widgets until the site was prepared for opening.

Now, we need to check how all our activity affected the appearance of the site pages and, if necessary, correct everything that is required.

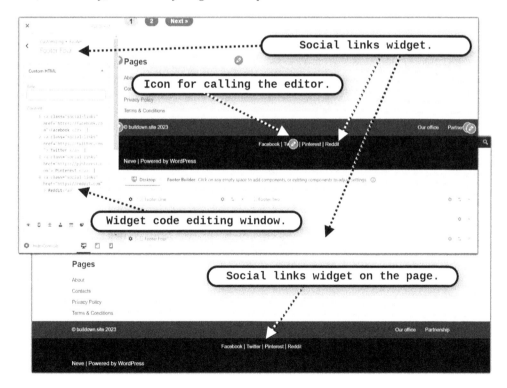

Figure 5-20. An example of a social links text widget.

5.6. Checking the Visual Structure of the Site

5.6.1. Why and How to Check Pages of Various Types

Treat this work as the final stage of site structuring.

Consider that at this stage, you are dealing with the visualization of the internal structure of the site or even just its visual structuring.

This work is not very difficult, but it is vital. Here, we will have to spend some time performing practical tests of the functioning of the site.

Once you have completed this work, you'll have just one labor-intensive step left to complete the site creation: filling the site with content.

Here's what the work involves and how it should be done.

5.6.2. Testing Menus and Checking Layouts

We need to click on all menu items and visually check the layouts of the category pages. It means exactly what it says and nothing more.

As long as the site only has a small amount of content published, it won't take much time.

Each page you open needs to be checked for each type of device - desktop, tablet, and phone.

Don't try to do this on the *Appearance* settings pages in the *WordPress* interface!

Open actual website pages and check how they look. All parameters of the appearance of pages and elements matter!

It is best to temporarily disable the blocking plugin, clear the cache, and use the browser in incognito mode. In this case, you will see the accurate picture. To simulate different devices, simply resize the browser window to fit the width; the effect will be the one you need.

You may ask - why do you need to spend time on this, since pages of all categories will work exactly the same as any of them?

For now, take my word for it: if the structure and scale of the site still allow you to subject it to total control, do not miss this opportunity. There are quite a few reasons for this, and the unlikely possibility that a category page will not work as expected is only one of them.

Subject the results of all you have created and tuned to the strictest check!

At the initial stage of creating a website, this can give you a variety of results. In the future, you will thank yourself more than once for doing this work.

I can accurately predict one of them: most of you, when thoroughly checking the site, will experience approximately the same sensations that occur when re-reading a serious and complicated book.

You'll discover things you hadn't noticed before, and you'll come up with ideas for improving your site that weren't there before.

When this happens, you'll remember what I just told you.

Of course, during such a check, you may find some shortcomings and errors. Now, you have enough knowledge and experience to return to the required step of work and fix everything.

5.6.2. Checklist for Final Inspection

1. After checking the correctness of menu items and visual control of layouts, check all the widgets that are already on the site. Widgets should be in the right places and look the way you configured them.
2. Official and other necessary pages. Open them all one by one using links in widgets or footer menus. Make sure each one is in the right place and has the correct name and the correct slug.
3. If you have already managed to hide unnecessary fields and add a message about copyright in the footer of the site, check how it looks, whether everything was done without errors, and whether everything is displayed as needed.
4. Check the title and description metadata in the site page codes. They must be there.
5. If you have already installed and activated the PRO version of the SEO plugin, also check for the presence of a scheme called "breadcrumbs", in the page codes. Are you not ready to perform such actions? It's okay, we'll talk about this in more detail when preparing the website for the opening.

With this, we have completed the main work of creating the internal structure of the site and customizing its presentation on its pages. All the small improvements that we postponed at the stage of preparing the site for opening will be completed after filling the site with content.

After you fill the site with content, return to the stage of customizing the appearance of the pages and check everything again.

In the future, as the site fills up, you will no longer have the need for such strict control, neither the physical ability to check hundreds of pages, nor the need for this.

To be honest, you won't have such a desire either. You will already know your site well, and the likelihood of some random error will only decrease as you continue to work on it.

And you will be able to devote much more of your time to what you created your site for - working on its content.

We will consider all the main issues related to content creation at the next stage of work on the site.

Stage Results

We have just completed one of the most important stages of working on the site. Honestly, since we try not to be distracted and not to study anything unnecessary or unnecessary, this stage is just as important as all the previous and all subsequent ones.

There is one crucial difference: the site's structure will necessarily grow and become more complex as the site is filled with content.

Therefore, it is vital to correctly create the basic structure of the site from the very beginning since it will be almost impossible to redo it.

We got an idea of the internal structure of the site and its connection with the external presentation on the site pages and learned what taxonomies are and what types of taxonomies are currently used and necessary for each site.

We found out what categories and tags are, what is the difference between them, what they are used for, and how they should be presented on the pages of the site.

We learned how to create categories and tags, add and edit their names, slugs, descriptions, metatags, and illustrations for SEO, as well as add versions of titles, descriptions, and illustrations for use on social networks.

We learned what formal pages a site should and can contain and what information should be placed on them.

We studied various types of site menus, and learned their features, purpose, and methods of placement on the site. We created the main menu of the site and added categories and a link to the main page. We created a footer menu and added to it links to the official pages of the site.

After all this, we performed a detailed check of the layout settings of the main page, category pages, and post pages. We checked the functioning of the menu and made sure that the navigation through its items was correct.

Complete all stage work on your site listed above and, as usual, record everything you've done in the Planner.

Afterword

Did you read this book carefully, repeat exactly all the actions described in it, did not skip the explanations, and even compared screenshots from the book with what you saw on the screen?

This means that the world will never be the same for you.

You have accomplished something that just recently seemed unthinkable and impossible to you.

You have registered a domain name, linked it to hosting, configured files and folders on the server, connected an SSL certificate, created a database, created a user account for this database and granted it the required permissions, downloaded the WordPress distribution, prepared to install it, installed WordPress, logged into the WordPress system on your own website, studied the system interface, made all the necessary system settings, installed and configured the necessary plugins, installed block and classic themes, studied the theme settings system, made the necessary site design settings, created official pages, created and edited categories and tags and understood the difference between them, carried out internal and external structuring of the main elements of all pages of the site, checked its functioning and eliminated the shortcomings found.

Did I forget to mention anything?

It is quite possible that this tedious list is incomplete, but that does not matter. It simply lists the most essential tasks that you were able to complete on your own to create your own website successfully.

When you first picked up this book, you didn't have a website.

Now, you have it. Now, you can't wait to show it to the world. Everyone should like it, right? It will definitely attract attention and get a lot of traffic! It simply cannot help but earn a ton, a mountain of money!

Of course, all this is possible. You just need to do a few more things and be patient. You have successfully started your journey, and now you need to continue it. Do not stop!

Now, you need to create content. We'll tackle this together in the next book.

List of Illustrations

Figure title	Paragraph
Figure 1-1. Choosing and Registering a Domain Name.	1.1.2
Figure 1-2. Domain Names and Website Hosting Services.	1.2.1
Figure 1-3. cPanel Access Method.	1.2.2
Figure 1-4. The cPanel Interface and access to the File Manager app.	1.2.3
Figure 1-5. Three ways to access the root directory of the website.	1.2.3
Figure 1-6. Root domain and additional domains folders.	1.2.3
Figure 1-7. Changing File Manager preferences to display hidden files.	1.2.3
Figure 1-8. Access to nameserver data - various options exist.	1.3.1
Figure 1-9. Changing nameservers names - an option.	1.3.2
Figure 1-10. Check domain availability using the Windows console.	1.4.2
Figure 1-11. Creating a text file in the website's root directory.	1.4.4
Figure 1-12. Editing and saving a text file with the File Manager.	1.4.4
Figure 1-13. Invoking the domain zone record settings page.	1.5.1
Figure 1-14. Invoking the Zone Editor in cPanel.	1.5.2
Figure 1-15. List of website versions and installed SSL certificates.	1.6.1
Figure 1-16. Forced activation of an SSL certificate.	1.6.2
Figure 1-17. Checking access to a test file using a secure protocol.	1.6.3
Figure 1-18. Browser window with information about the SSL certificate.	1.6.3
Figure 1-19. Creating the .htaccess file.	1.7
Figure 1-20. Checking redirection to access a test file via a secure protocol.	1.7
Figure 1-21. Creating a new database for the future site.	1.8.1
Figure 1-22. Creating a new database user for the future site.	1.8.2
Figure 1-23. Granting privileges to the database user.	1.8.3
Figure 1-24. General information about databases and their users.	1.8.3
Figure 1-25. Interface to access database operations.	1.8.3
Figure 2-1. Uploading the WordPress archive to the root directory	2.1.1
Figure 2-2. Unpacking the WordPress archive in the root directory	2.1.2
Figure 2-3. Selecting WordPress directories and files.	2.1.2
Figure 2-4. Moving selected WordPress directories and files.	2.1.2
Figure 2-5. Modifying the wp-config-sample.php file.	2.2.2
Figure 2-6. Getting started with the Website Development Planner.	2.3.1
Figure 2-7. WordPress installer window with language selection dialog.	2.3.2
Figure 2-8. WordPress installer window with registration information fields.	2.3.2
Figure 2-9. WordPress installer window showing completion notification.	2.3.2
Figure 2-10. WordPress login window.	2.3.3
Figure 2-11. WordPress system interface with a link to the homepage.	2.3.3
Figure 2-12. Home page of a newly created website.	2.3.3
Figure 2-13. The WordPress system interface of a newly created website.	2.4.2
Figure 2-14. The Dashboard/ Updates block interface.	2.4.2
Figure 2-15. Main menu of the system.	2.4.2
Figure 2-16. Top toolbar, WordPress interface.	2.4.3
Figure 2-17. Top toolbar, website homepage.	2.4.3
Figure 2-18. Top panel with screen options.	2.4.3
Figure 2-19. The main work/ content area.	2.4.3

Figure 2-20. The right sidebar area.   2.4.3
Figure 2-21. Settings/ Reading page.   2.5.1
Figure 2-22. Settings/ Writing page.   2.5.3
Figure 2-23. Settings/ Discussion page.   2.5.3
Figure 2-24. Settings/ Media page.   2.5.3
Figure 2-25. Settings/ Permalinks page.   2.5.3
Figure 2-26. Settings/ Privacy Policy page.   2.5.3
Figure 2-27. Tools/ Site Health page.   2.6.1
Figure 2-28. Plugins/ Installed Plugins page.   2.6.2
Figure 2-29. Appearance/Themes page.   2.6.3
Figure 2-30. Tools/ Site Health page after deleting themes and plugins.   2.6.4
Figure 2-31. Tools/ Site Health page, Info tab.   2.6.5
Figure 2-32. Measuring Core Web Vital scores using the Lighthouse.   2.6.6
Figure 2-33. Core Web Vitals scores measured with Lighthouse.   2.6.6
Figure 2-34. Accessing the website with various prefixes and protocols.   2.6.6
Figure 3-1.Users/ All Users.   3.1
Figure 3-2. Users/ All Users/ Profile.   3.1
Figure 3-3. WordPress Plugins/Add New: search and install the plugin.   3.3.1
Figure 3-4. WordPress Plugins/Add New: plugin activation.   3.3.1
Figure 3-5. Plugins/Installed Plugins/AIO WP Security, links to use.   3.3.1
Figure 3-6. WP Security/ Dashboard.   3.3.2
Figure 3-7. WP Security/ User Security.   3.3.2
Figure 3-8. WP Security/ User Security/ Manual Approval.   3.3.2
Figure 3-9. cPanel/Database phpMyAdmin page.   3.3.2
Figure 3-10. WP Security/ Database Security.   3.3.2
Figure 3-11. WP Security/ Dashboard: updated security score.   3.3.2
Figure 3-12. WP Security/ Filesystem Security.   3.3.2
Figure 3-13. WP Security/ Blacklist Manager.   3.3.2
Figure 3-14. WP Security/ Firewall/: Basic Firewall Rules.   3.3.2
Figure 3-15. WP Security/ Firewall/: Additional Firewall Rules.   3.3.2
Figure 3-16. WP Security/ Firewall/: 6G Blacklist firewall rules.   3.3.2
Figure 3-17. WP Security/ Firewall/: Internet bots.   3.3.2
Figure 3-18. WP Security/ Miscellaneous.   3.3.2
Figure 3-19. WP Security/ Tools.   3.3.2
Figure 3-20. WP Security/ Dashboard page: final security score   3.3.2
Figure 3-21. WP Security/ Settings page, settings export and import.   3.3.3
Figure 3-22. NinjaFirewall/ Firewall Policies.   3.3.4
Figure 3-23. NinjaFirewall/ Logs/ Firewall Log.   3.3.4
Figure 3-24. NinjaFirewall/ Logs/ Live Log.   3.3.4
Figure 3-25. NinjaFirewall/ Event Notifications.   3.3.4
Figure 3-26. NinjaScanner interface.   3.3.5
Figure 3-27. Nifty Coming Soon Page/ Options/ Themes.   3.4
Figure 3-28. Nifty Coming Soon Page/ Options.   3.4
Figure 3-29. Coming Soon Page/ Coming Soon Mode.   3.4
Figure 3-30. LiteSpeed Cache/ Cache/ Object.   3.5.1
Figure 3-31. Ways to access Autoptimize/ Settings.   3.5.2
Figure 3-32. Autoptimize/ Settings/ JS, CSS & HTML.   3.5.2
Figure 3-33. Autoptimize/ Settings/ Extra.   3.5.2

Figure 3-34. WordPress interface page with the Autoptimize toolbar.   3.5.2
Figure 3-35. Plugin search page with additional performance plugins.   3.5.3
Figure 3-36. installed SEO Press plugin and the left sidebar menu.   3.6.1
Figure 3-37. SEO Press plugin and link to its PRO version.   3.6.1
Figure 3-38. Installing the SEO Press PRO plugin from the archive.   3.6.2
Figure 3-39. SEO Press PRO license activation.   3.6.2
Figure 3-40. SEO/ Dashboard.   3.6.3
Figure 3-41. Search results for plugins with the word "Classic."   3.7
Figure 4-1. Theme searching page.   4.2.2
Figure 4-2. Chosen theme page.   4.2.3
Figure 4-3. Theme homepage sample with a switch of device type.   4.2.3
Figure 4-4. Core Web Vitals score for the demo page with the toolbar.   4.2.3
Figure 4-5. Core Web Vitals score for the demo page without the toolbar.   4.2.3
Figure 4-6. Installing the theme.   4.3.3
Figure 4-7. Activation of the theme.   4.3.3
Figure 4-8. The new look of the empty homepage of the website.   4.3.3
Figure 4-9. The homepage of the website filled with dummy content.   4.3.3
Figure 4-10. cPanel/ File Manager: creating a child theme folder.   4.4.2
Figure 4-11. Created style.css file.   4.4.2
Figure 4-12. Created functions.php file.   4.4.2
Figure 4-13. Appearance/ Themes page.   4.4.2
Figure 4-14. Temporarily disabling plugins and clearing caches.   4.5.1
Figure 4-15. The Appearance menu.   4.5.2
Figure 4-16. The Appearance/ Customize menu and page.   4.5.2
Figure 4-17. Appearance/Customize/Layout menu.   4.5.3
Figure 4-18. Appearance/ Customize/ Layout/ Container settings.   4.5.3
Figure 4-19. Appearance/ Customize/ Layout Content/ Sidebar settings.   4.5.3
Figure 4-20. Appearance/ Customize/ Layout/ Blog/ Archive settings.   4.5.3
Figure 4-21. Appearance/ Customize/ Layout/ Single Post settings.   4.5.3
Figure 4-22. Appearance/ Customize/ Layout/ Page settings.   4.5.3
Figure 4-23. Appearance/Customize/Header settings.   4.5.4
Figure 4-24. Appearance/ Customize/ Header/ Row: adding blocks.   4.5.4
Figure 4-25. Appearance/ Customize/ Header/ Primary Menu/ Settings.   4.5.4
Figure 4-26. Appearance/ Customize/ Header/ Primary Menu/ .../ General.   4.5.4
Figure 4-27. Appearance/ Customize/ Header/ Primary Menu/ .../ Layout.   4.5.4
Figure 4-28. Appearance/ Customize/ Header/ Primary Menu/ .../ Style.   4.5.4
Figure 4-29. Appearance/ Customize/ Header/ Row Settings.   4.5.4
Figure 4-30. Appearance/ Customize/ Header/ Mobile Sidebar menu.   4.5.4
Figure 4-31. Appearance/ Customize/ Header/ Mobile Sidebar/ Layout.   4.5.4
Figure 4-32. Appearance/ Customize/ Header/ Mobile Sidebar/ Style.   4.5.4
Figure 4-33. Appearance/Customize/Header/add button menu.   4.5.4
Figure 4-34. Appearance/ Customize/ Header/ Header Presets menu.   4.5.4
Figure 4-35. Activating settings using Shift-Click.   4.5.4
Figure 4-36. Appearance/ Customize/ Footer/ Available Components menu.   4.5.4
Figure 4-37. Appearance/ Customize/ Footer/ Footer One menu.   4.5.4
Figure 4-38. Appearance/ Customize/ Colors & Background menu.   4.5.5
Figure 4-39. Appearance/ Customize/ Typography/ General menu.   4.5.5
Figure 4-40. Appearance/ Customize/ Typography/ Headings menu.   4.5.5

Figure 4-41. Appearance/ Customize/ Typography/ Blog menu.   4.5.5
Figure 4-42. Appearance/Customize/Buttons menu.   4.5.5
Figure 4-43. Appearance/Customize/Form Fields menu.   4.5.5
Figure 4-44. Inspecting screenshot to find and copy a class name.   4.6.2.1
Figure 4-45. The page with a hidden element.   4.6.2.1
Figure 4-46. The classic theme page on the official website.   4.7.1
Figure 4-47. Appearance/Customize: general settings.   4.7.2
Figure 4-48. Appearance/Widget options.   4.7.2
Figure 4-49. Widget settings using the Widget Options plugin, an example.   4.7.3
Figure 5-1. Linking a post to a category and tags.   5.1.2
Figure 5-2. Categories/ Add New Category page: creating a category   5.2.1
Figure 5-3. Categories/ Add New Category page: creating a nested category.   5.2.1
Figure 5-4. Categories/ "Uncategorized" category.   5.2.1
Figure 5-5. Settings/ Writing page: changing the default category.   5.2.1
Figure 5-6. Categories/ "Uncategorized" category removing.   5.2.1
Figure 5-7. Categories page: a list of website categories.   5.2.3
Figure 5-8. Edit Category page.   5.2.3
Figure 5-9. Edit Category page/ SEO metabox.   5.2.4
Figure 5-10. Tags page: a list of website tags.   5.3.1
Figure 5-11. Edit Tag page.   5.3.2
Figure 5-12. Edit Tag page/ SEO metabox.   5.3.4
Figure 5-13. The Page URL example.   5.4.1
Figure 5-14. Links to obligatory pages in the footer menu.   5.4.6
Figure 5-15. Appearance/ Menus page.   5.5.1
Figure 5-16. Appearance/ Customize/ Menus page.   5.5.1
Figure 5-17. Appearance/ Menus/ Main Menu page.   5.5.2
Figure 5-18. Appearance/ Menus/ Secondary Menu page.   5.5.3
Figure 5-19. Appearance/ Menus/ Footer Menu page.   5.5.4
Figure 5-20. An example of a social links text widget.   5.5.5

www.ingramcontent.com/pod-product-compliance
Lightning Source LLC
LaVergne TN
LVHW051233050326
832903LV00028B/2386